# Seasonal
# Secrets

from

COOKING WITH CLASS

VICTORIA O'NEILL

*Best wishes*
*Victoria*

VICTORIA O'NEILL
COOKING WITH CLASS

First published in Great Britain in 2011
by Cooking with Class Ltd, Pyon House, Herefordshire.


Copyright © Cooking with Class Ltd 2011

Text copyright © Victoria O'Neill

Photographs copyright © Victoria O'Neill

Front cover, back cover flap and Cooking with Class photographs
by Richard Weaver Photography www.richardweaverphotography.co.uk

ISBN 978-0-9570641-0-2

A CIP catalogue record for this book is available from the British Library.

While all reasonable care has been taken during the preparation of this edition, neither the
publisher, author, nor editor can accept responsibility for any consequences arising from
the use thereof or from the information contained therein.

Design: Marsh Court Design, Hereford. marshcourt@tiscali.co.uk

Printed and bound by Orphans Press Ltd, Leominster, Herefordshire.

# Contents

This book is dedicated
to the memory of my husband,
Roger Anthony Arthur Leech.

## Acknowledgements

This book's inspiration is largely due to my students and the feedback that they volunteer. For a cookery teacher, it is always flattering to hear that a recipe you have taught has become a favourite dish for your students. But, more importantly, it is great to hear that they enjoy and succeed at cooking.

I would like to thank:

all the people who encouraged me to write this book, especially my daughter Frances and my son Felix, who are always supportive and also good critics and accomplished cooks themselves.

friends and family, both here in the UK and in Australia who have chivvied me along from far away or from closer quarters, and supported me through the stressful times.

those who worked on the creation of this book, especially Susan Harris, without whom the design and production would never have happened, and Marie-Noëlle Witty, whose editorial and proof-reading skills gave me the courage to embark on this project.

Thanks also to my local suppliers, Jason, the fishmonger, James the butcher, and all those at the local farmers' market.

# Foreword

Throughout my career, I have met hundreds of excellent cooks but few with the talent and flair of Victoria. She cooks instinctively and with passion and that passion is infectious.

I have had the pleasure to visit and demonstrate several times at Canon Pyon and have observed a true professional who demonstrates and teaches seasonal, practical recipes at her classes. It is obvious that the moment the class is over everyone can't wait to get home and try them.

Here she transforms traditional recipes and adapts exotic dishes for everyday life. This book deserves a place in your kitchen.

Mary Berry

# Introduction

*Seasonal Secrets* brings together some of the most popular recipes from *Cooking with Class* at Pyon House in Herefordshire. Inspired by my students and the feedback they volunteer, I wrote this book to share with you the many good reasons for preparing food at home, despite our busy lives. I believe passionately that cooking is primarily a pleasure, not a chore and that by concentrating on seasonal ingredients, food will always be exciting.

Often, when I am thinking what to cook for friends and family, I look through my kitchen window to the vegetable garden beyond and find there the starting point for what to make. In the winter with leeks and the elegant cavolo nero cabbage surviving the weather I can plan hearty and sustaining dishes. When spring comes I look eagerly to see the tarragon resurfacing, and enjoy lighter, fresh tasting dishes enhanced by young herbs. Summer brings a complete change of ingredients with spinach, tomatoes and apricots – which is part of the fun of thinking and cooking seasonally. Salad leaves are all in season, as well as the jewel-like summer fruits. With the approach of autumn, fruit trees laden with apples, quinces and damsons inspire luscious desserts and opportunities to fill the pantry with home-made jams and chutneys.

From the southern hemisphere to Herefordshire via Italy, France and the British Isles, the flavours and influences in these recipes also reflect my life in cooking.

Growing up in Sydney, with its multi cultural culinary influences, and encouraged by my mother, I was baking cakes at eight and curries a few years later. In my early twenties I travelled to London to attend the *Cordon Bleu* cookery school. The techniques I learned there have stood me in good stead for the rest of my life and opened the door to years of globe-trotting cooking – roast grouse with game chips for grand Scottish shooting parties, French food for an Italian Baronessa in Venice, Aussie meat pies with posh fillings, and cakes for Dame Joan Sutherland – cooking has truly been my passport.

When I moved back to Australia, *Cooking with Class* had its first incarnation in Sydney. I used to take my students early in the morning, to the fish market, or the butcher or greengrocer, introducing them to the delights of discovering seasonal produce and getting to know the specialist shopkeepers. We would then spend the morning cooking what we had bought. Gathering ingredients, whether from the garden or from markets and shops, has for me always been intimately connected with the dishes I create.

In 1985 I married Roger and before long we moved *Cooking with Class* to England: first to Oxfordshire and then to Herefordshire – its home for the last 16 years. Our children Frances and Felix have both taught me a whole new strand of cooking: the life of the family cook. Cooking for – or rather, with – them led to my classes for children. Now in their early twenties, Felix is the master of Tiramisu (*see p146*) and all things Japanese, and Frances is studying patisserie in France and has a wonderful food blog at www.tangerinedrawings.com. Roger, who died nearly five years ago, would have loved to have seen all this and to have read this book, and I would love still to be making him his favourites – roast pork and gooseberry crumble cake.

Seasons change... but wherever you live in the world I hope this book will become a constant reminder of how to enjoy and succeed at cooking.

Do get in touch and let me know how you get on with the recipes – or tell me at a class!

Victoria O'Neill

*victoria@cookingwithclass.co.uk*

# Spring

# Spring taglierini
## SERVES 4

*Spring's green colour is everywhere and nowhere more than in the kitchen garden. My tarragon has reappeared, the English spinach is germinating and I have plenty of chard going mad, growing tall and fast going to seed along with the leeks. So what better way to celebrate spring, than with an* impromptu *spring pasta dish?*

*It is important to buy the best Italian dried pasta you can find. Ask any Italian – they wouldn't compromise on pasta quality. I like* De Cecco *and* Buitoni *pasta which is readily available in supermarkets. Taglierini are very thin noodles, less robust than spaghetti, so they make a lighter dish altogether.*

200 g (7 oz) taglierini
   (4 bundles)

1 bunch spring onions

150 g (5½ oz) shelled broad
   beans (3 times their
   weight unshelled)

150 g (5½ oz) shelled peas
   (twice their weight
   unshelled)

150 g (5½ oz) spinach
   leaves

1-2 tbs fresh tarragon

50-100 g (1¾ - 3½ oz)
   butter

salt and pepper

**GARNISH**

100 g (3½ oz) grated
   Parmesan cheese

Prepare the vegetables. Tear up large spinach leaves and slice the spring onions. Mix in a bowl with the peas and broad beans.

Cook the taglierini in a large saucepan of boiling salted water until *al dente*. Check the packet's instructions (usually about 2-5 minutes). Add the vegetables to the pasta pot in the last few minutes of the pasta's cooking time. Drain the cooked pasta and vegetables but don't throw all the water away.

In a broad sauté pan, heat the butter and the chopped herbs. When the butter starts to sizzle, add the pasta with the vegetables to the pan and heat gently, adding in a little of the grated Parmesan cheese and a little of the pasta water to make a sauce.

If you think the sauce is too dry, add a little more of the water. This will help to both heat the pasta and continue to cook it. Season well with black pepper.

Divide between four warm plates. Grate over a little Parmesan cheese and serve.

# Asparagus crèpes with pine nut and olive dressing
**SERVES 4+**

*The local asparagus season is short, so if you enjoy this delicious vegetable, make the most of it. No apologies for having two asparagus recipes. The punchy flavours of olives, pine nuts and feta cheese complement asparagus in a surprising way. Making crèpes is easy to master. You will need a good light-weight crèpe pan, a 50 g (2 oz) ladle and a palette knife.*

## CRÈPES
100 g (3½ oz) plain flour

pinch salt

1 egg

300 ml (½ pt) milk and
   water mixed

butter

200 g (7 oz) mild feta
   cheese

2 tbs olive oil

2 bunches asparagus

## DRESSING
30 g (1 oz) pine nuts,
   toasted

100 ml (3½ fl oz) olive oil

1 tbs wine vinegar

50 g (1¾ oz) black olives

Whisk the flour, salt and egg together in a bowl with half the milk. Beat out the lumps before adding the remaining milk. Melt a knob of butter in a crèpe pan, swirl it around to cover the pan, then pour the excess into the crèpe mixture. Get the pan really hot, then away from the heat, ladle in a little of the batter. Swizzle the pan, so that the batter covers the surface evenly.

Return the pan to the heat, and as the edge of the crèpe browns, run around it with the end of a palette knife. When you think the crèpe is cooked enough, slide the palette knife under the top third and turn the crèpe over. Cook the second side for a few seconds then tip the crèpe onto a cooling rack. Repeat until you have 8-12 crèpes. (Any extra crèpes can be frozen for another day).

Wash the asparagus well, then break off and discard the tough ends. Lay the spears in a frying pan with a 1 cm (½") of water and a sprinkling of salt. Cover with a lid and steam over a medium heat until partially cooked. Take them out of the pan to drain and cool.

Lay out 8-12 crèpes and crumble over a little feta cheese. Divide the asparagus between the crèpes and then roll them up.

Place the rolled crèpes in a single layer on a buttered ovenproof dish and drizzle with a little oil. Bake uncovered at 180°C (350°F, gas 4) for 10-15 minutes or until heated through and the crèpes are slightly crisp. In an Aga, place in the middle of the roasting oven for 10-15 minutes.

Chop the pine nuts and olives, place in a bowl and stir in the olive oil and vinegar. Serve the warm crèpes, spooning over the olive dressing.

# Asparagus with smoked salmon

SERVES 4-6

2 bunches fresh asparagus

butter

salt and coarsely ground
   pepper

200 g (7 oz) smoked
   salmon

Prepare the washed asparagus by breaking off and discarding the tough bases. Place them in a broad frying pan, add 1 cm (½") water, sprinkle with a little salt and cover with a lid. Steam until cooked. This will take about 5 minutes.

Drain the asparagus and place it on warm plates. Melt a little butter in the pan and then pour it over the asparagus. Sprinkle liberally with coarsely ground pepper.

Tear up the sliced smoked salmon and scatter over the asparagus. Serve immediately.

# Corn bread with scrambled egg

SERVES 4

*Eggs are a powerful symbol of spring and indeed Easter. Scrambled eggs make a good brunch or supper dish and if you make this corn bread to go with them it takes the whole meal out of the ordinary.*

## CORN BREAD

150 g (5½ oz) self-raising flour

1 tbs caster sugar

2 tsp baking powder

1 tsp salt

100 g (3½ oz) fine polenta (maize meal)

50 g (1¾ oz) grated Cheddar cheese

½ cup chopped fresh herbs

2 eggs

250 ml (9 fl oz) natural live yoghurt

75 ml (2¾ fl oz) sunflower oil

## SCRAMBLED EGG

8 eggs

200 ml (7 fl oz) whipping cream

salt and pepper

To make the corn bread, mix all the dry ingredients together in a bowl. Add the eggs, yoghurt and oil and then stir to make a batter.

Pour into a 500 g (1 lb) loaf tin that has been greased with a little oil or lined with baking / silicone paper. Bake at 180°C (350°F, gas 4) for 45 minutes until set. In an Aga, place on the bottom shelf of the the roasting oven with the heat shield above. Test with a skewer to see if it is dry in the centre.

For the scrambled eggs, beat the eggs and cream together and season well with salt and pepper. Cook in a non-stick frying pan over a low heat, stirring continually until the egg starts to set. Don't overcook them. Stop cooking and stirring just before you think it is ready. The eggs will keep on cooking in the heat of the pan, so if you take them off the heat now and serve them, they will be perfect.

Serve the scrambled eggs with thick slices of warm corn bread.

## GETTING AHEAD

Bake the bread the day before and lightly toast slices to go with the eggs.

# Razor clams with anchovy butter

**SERVES 4**

*When I go to the fishmonger I like to seize upon whatever is newly in season, so in May I am likely to find razor clams. These long shells are basically prepared and cooked in the same way as mussels; washed well and steamed open with seasonings. Like mussels, they should be closed when live and should not be eaten if they don't open after cooking. They are delicious, especially when served hot with anchovy butter.*

12 razor clams

2 tbs olive oil

2 shallots

2 celery stalks

½ a glass of white wine

salt and pepper

**ANCHOVY BUTTER**

25 g (1 oz) anchovy fillets

50 g (1¾ oz) unsalted butter

½ tsp lemon juice

pepper

**TO SERVE**

washed salad leaves

a little extra olive oil

Wash the clams in cold water to dislodge any grit. Peel and slice the shallots and slice the celery. Place the vegetables in a saucepan big enough to fit all the razors. Add the olive oil and start to sweat the vegetables over a medium heat. When they start to turn translucent, add the clams and then cover with a lid. Increase the heat and steam until the shells open. This will take less than 5 minutes. Then remove the pan from the heat.

For the anchovy butter, squash the anchovies and butter together in a mortar and pestle. Add a little lemon juice and pepper to taste.

Divide the salad between plates and drizzle over a little olive oil. Take the hot clams out of the shells, place on the salad and dab anchovy butter on top.

Serve as a lunch dish or as a first course.

# Goat cheese and pear tartlets
## SERVES 4

*There are certain dishes that teenage girls like and this was one of Frances' favourites
when she was younger. Apart from loving goat cheese, I think the ingenious way
of forming the tart shapes appealed to her. If you prefer, use a different soft cheese
e.g. Gorgonzola or even Philadelphia.*

250 g (9 oz) ready-made
puff pastry

100 g (3½ oz) soft goat
cheese

1 egg

1 tbs crème fraîche

1 tbs chopped fresh thyme

2 ripe pears e.g. William
pears

Roll the pastry to a 30 cm (12") square. Using a sharp knife,
trim away the edge of the pastry. Draw the point of a sharp
knife through the pastry to do this; don't cut down or you will
squash the many layers of pastry together making it difficult for
the pastry to rise effectively. Now cut the pastry into 4 equal
squares. On each square make two L shaped cuts in the
pastry 1 cm (½") in from the edge, leaving the two opposite
corners uncut.

To form the walls of the tartlet cases, brush the edges of the
pastry with water and lift up one cut corner and draw it across
the pastry to the opposite side. Repeat with the opposite
corner. Press the edges firmly to seal. Place the tartlet cases
on a damp baking sheet. Prick the base of each tart with a fork
and refrigerate until ready to cook.

Bake the pastry cases for 5-8 minutes, at 200°C (400°F, gas 6)
or put the tray directly on the floor of the Aga's roasting oven.
Bake until puffed and golden. Cool slightly before gently
pushing down the pastry bases.

Peel and cut the pears in half, cutting out the cores. Lay one
half, cut side down, in each pastry case.

Beat together the goat cheese, crème fraîche, egg and thyme.
Season with salt and pepper. Spoon the mixture over the
pears and bake in the middle of the hot oven for 10 minutes or
until just set.

Serve warm as a first course, or with a little dressed salad as a
main meal.

## GETTING AHEAD
Fill the pastries and refrigerate them until ready to bake.

# A little spring salad with butterflake rolls

SERVES 4

*Make the most of spring vegetables with a very simple salad served with fresh bread.*

½ a bag of mixed salad leaves, or better still, salad from the garden

1 punnet cherry tomatoes, halved

a handful purple sprouting broccoli, steamed

4 cooked artichoke hearts from a jar or home-prepared

12 radishes, halved

8 quails eggs or 2 hens eggs, hard boiled and peeled

DRESSING

3 tbs sunflower oil

1½ tsp wine vinegar

¼ tsp French mustard

1 tsp fresh, chopped herbs, e.g. parsley, thyme

salt and pepper

Whisk the dressing together and pour over the salad leaves. Toss with your hands and divide between 4 plates.

Scatter all the vegetables between the plates and top with the chopped eggs. Serve with freshly baked butter flake rolls.

To prepare fresh artichoke hearts, pick (or buy) them small, no bigger than 7 cm / 3". Cut off and discard the top half of the artichokes. Pull away any hard outside leaves. The remaining outside leaves should have their tops snipped off if they feel hard and coarse. Cut the artichokes in half, rubbing all the cut surfaces with lemon. Wash the artichokes well, then steam or boil them until tender – about 15 minutes – and then drain and cut the artichoke hearts into quarters. Whilst still warm, toss them in a little olive oil and lemon juice, and season with salt and pepper. They will keep, covered, in the fridge for several days.

# Butterflake rolls

## 12 ROLLS

*These little rolls are an elegant accompaniment, consisting of buttery layers that the diner can peel apart. Bread making skills are acquired through practice, not a hard task and infinitely rewarding as you provide flavoursome home made bread to an always appreciative audience. So, if you're not used to making bread, I can only urge you to start here with this recipe. Hopefully you will get caught up with your creativity.*

175 ml (6 fl oz) warm water

250 g (9 oz) strong white flour

1¼ tsp fast action dried yeast

¾ tsp sugar

¼ tsp salt

1½ tbs powdered milk

15 g (½ oz) soft butter, about the size of a walnut

**TO FINISH**

extra 50 g (1¾ oz) melted butter

Measure all the dry ingredients into a bowl and mix together. Pour in the hand-warm water all at once and stir, adding the softened butter as the dough comes together. Tip onto a lightly floured surface and knead the dough by hand until the butter is absorbed and the dough is elastic. This will take between 5-10 minutes. Put the dough back in the bowl, cover with cling film and leave to rise for 1 hour in a warm place.

Roll the dough out thinly into a rectangle, approximately 20 x 26 cm (8" x 10"). Brush with the extra melted butter. Cut into 2½ cm (1") strips, then stack 5-6 strips on top of each other. Cut off sections of the dough at 2½ cm (1") intervals.

Place the pieces, end up, in greased mince pie tins and leave to double in size for about 20-30 minutes.

Bake until golden – 15-20 minutes at 200°C (400°F, gas 6). In an Aga, bake in the middle of the roasting oven.

# Crispy baked bream with garlic and rosemary
**SERVES 4**

*There is something special about the Italians and their use of flavours. Would I have thought of putting rosemary with fish? Combined with salt and gutsy olives, this dish really does have that* umami *factor. The crumbs underneath absorb all the fish juices – giving a crunch reminiscent of fried fish, but healthier. I serve buttered samphire and fondant potatoes with the fish. You can find samphire at the fishmongers when in season.*

4 fillets of fish e.g. black bream or sea bass fillets

pepper

2 cloves of garlic, cut in thin slices

leaves of 4 sprigs of rosemary

1½ cups dried breadcrumbs

1 tsp flaked (Maldon) sea salt

50 g (1¾ oz) stoned black olives

olive oil

GARNISH

samphire

fondant potatoes

chopped fresh tomato salad

Season the fillets all over with salt and pepper. Make 3 slits in the skin side and insert the rosemary leaves and garlic slivers.

Grease a baking sheet and sprinkle the breadcrumbs in 4 patches the size of each fillet. Grind over some salt and scatter the olives on the crumbs. Place the fillets on top of the breadcrumbs and drizzle with olive oil.

Bake at 200°C (400°F, gas 6) for 10 minutes. In an Aga, slide the baking sheet into the top of the roasting oven.

To serve, carefully lift the fillets with their crumb bases onto warm plates. Serve with washed samphire, tossed in a hot pan with melted butter for a few minutes to heat through. Accompany with fondant potatoes and tomato salad.

To make fondant potatoes, slice 4 medium sized old potatoes thinly. Put them in a saucepan and barely cover with half water, half milk. Season them with salt and cook gently with the lid on until the potatoes are soft and the liquid absorbed – approximately 10 minutes. Don't stir the pot or the potatoes will disintegrate.

**GETTING AHEAD**
Have the fish fully prepared on the baking sheet ready to pop in the oven.

# Beef rib with shallot sauce

**SERVES 4**

*This is a quick and succulent way to cook a rib of beef. In Herefordshire, we are spoiled with many good butchers and local farms who supply them. One of my favourites is beef from Risbury Court near Leominster which is aged for about 28 days, by my butcher James. It's a treat well worth the occasional indulgence.*

1 rib (1.5 kg / 3 lb 5 oz) of beef on the bone

½ tsp salt

1 tbs coarsely crushed peppercorns

2 tbs olive oil

2 tbs butter

4 shallots

200 ml (7 fl oz) red wine

4 tbs stock

salt & pepper

pinch of sugar

**TO SERVE**

steamed new potatoes

Trim the meat, getting rid of excess fat. Season the beef generously with the salt and the crushed peppercorns.

Preheat the oven to 240°C (430°F, gas 9). Heat a frying pan (that can go in the oven) until it is very hot. Add the oil and butter, and as it melts, add the beef, letting it brown on both sides for a total of 10 minutes. Place the pan in the oven, with the rib on its side for 15 minutes for medium rare, 25 minutes for well done.

Remove the beef from the pan and keep it warm for 10 minutes, while making the sauce.

Pour away the excess fat from the beef pan, slice the shallots and add them to the pan with the wine. Boil vigorously until the sauce has reduced by two thirds. Add the stock and any juices from the standing beef. Simmer to thicken further. Check the seasoning.

To serve, carve the meat on a board, cutting away the bone. Cut the beef into thick slices, across the grain. Place it on a serving dish and pour over the sauce.

# Beef rib with black bean sauce

SERVES 4

*This is a variation on the beef with shallots. Asian food relies a lot on store cupboard condiments – and if you have them, they make it easy to turn a few ingredients into something very flavoursome.*

**MARINADE**

½ cup sherry

4 tbs oyster sauce

2 tbs caster sugar

2 tbs *Kepac manis* (sweetened soy from Indonesia)

1 tbs sesame oil

1 tbs fish sauce

1 rib x 1.5 kg (3 lb 5 oz) of beef

2 tbs dried black beans

1 clove garlic, crushed

1 tbs soy sauce

1 tsp caster sugar

2 tbs water

1 tbs sherry

1 tsp sesame oil

**TO SERVE**

steamed winter or Chinese greens

Trim the beef as in the preceding recipe.

Mix all the marinade ingredients together. Spread the marinade all over the rib and leave to marinate for an hour.

For the sauce, soak the black beans for 10 minutes in half a cup of hot water and then drain. Place them in a small saucepan with the other sauce ingredients and heat through.

Cook the beef as in the preceding recipe.

Carve the beef and serve with the sauce and steamed greens.

# Pan-fried haddock and calamari with tartare sauce
SERVES 4

*Fish needs to be cooked quickly and simply. Accompaniments such as vegetables and sauces need to be prepared first so that everything is ready when the fish is cooked. Making mayonnaise with a hand-held blender is simple and your own tartare sauce will be really worth eating.*

300 g (10½ oz) cleaned
squid

400 g (14 oz) haddock fillet

salt and pepper

1-2 tbs sunflower oil

**TARTARE SAUCE**

1 whole egg

1 tsp French mustard

a big pinch of salt

1 tsp white wine vinegar

200 ml (7 fl oz) oil
(1/3 olive + 2/3 sunflower)

1 tbs each chopped
gherkins and capers

1 tbs each chopped parsley
and chives

a quarter of a shallot,
chopped

To make mayonnaise with a hand-held blender, put one whole egg, the mustard, salt and vinegar in the bottom of the beaker or narrow jug. Pour all the oil on top. Place the blender head firmly on the base of the container over the egg. Turn on the blender, but don't raise it at all until you can see that half the oil has turned into mayonnaise. When this has happened, lift the head up and down, with the motor running to finish blending in the oil. Adjust the seasoning and stir all the remaining tartare sauce ingredients into the mayonnaise.

Cut the haddock into neat 7 cm (3") pieces, cutting away any bone. Cut the squid into rings and season.

Heat a frying pan with a little sunflower oil and, when really hot, sear the haddock, flesh side down, cooking it until golden. Turn the fish over and cook for a further few minutes. The fish is cooked when it looks opaque and flakes when prodded. Remove the fish from the pan and keep it warm.

Reheat the pan with a little more oil and, when hot, stir-fry the squid rings and tentacles in batches. When the rings are golden, turn them and cook for a few minutes more. If squid is cooked quickly it will stay tender. Cook the squid in small batches so that the heat in the pan is retained. Drain it on kitchen paper.

Serve the haddock and calamari rings with the tartare sauce. Accompany with a good mixed salad.

**NOTE**

To clean squid, grab the head firmly and pull it away from the body. Cut off the tentacles below the eyes and reserve them. Pull out the transparent quill from the body and any mucky insides. Wash the squid tube, drain it and then slice it up. Pat rings dry with kitchen paper.

# Ham with spring vegetables

**SERVES 6**

*I have a great crop of mint outside my back door, which makes it easy to grab by the handful for making mint tea. I don't know why the leaves are so huge but they make a very alluring plant. For me, when the mint starts to reappear, it is a sign that spring is well on its way. This is an easy dish – served in one pot. It makes a comforting family meal, quite delicious with the ham and vegetables enveloped in a creamy sauce.*

700 g (1 lb 9 oz) cooked ham – one big thick slice

300 ml (½ pt) chicken or vegetable stock

4 leeks

2 celery sticks

150 g (5½ oz) shelled peas

2 spring onions

2-3 tbs fresh mint

1 tbs butter

2 tbs flour

150 ml (5 fl oz) crème fraîche or double cream

400 g (14 oz) new potatoes

Wash the leeks and celery and cut them into small batons. Place in a large pan and season with salt and pepper. Add half a cup of water and cook, covered with a lid, so they are effectively steaming. When they are tender, strain, retaining the liquid.

Wash, trim and chop the spring onions. In a separate saucepan, simmer the peas for 3 minutes with the spring onions.

Tear the ham into good sized pieces. Melt the butter in the large saucepan and stir in the flour. Remove from the heat and then gradually whisk in the stock. Reheat, continuing to whisk as the sauce thickens. Simmer for 5 minutes and then stir in the crème fraîche or cream.

Steam the potatoes until cooked.

Add the ham and vegetables to the sauce and then check the seasoning. The ham may have made the sauce salty enough. Reheat and stir in the chopped mint. Serve with the steamed potatoes.

**NOTE**

If the weather is hot, replace the sauce with 3 or 4 tablespoons of mayonnaise and serve the ham cold, on a bed of salad leaves.

**GETTING AHEAD**

The ham finished in the sauce can be prepared well ahead of time and reheated when needed.

# Leg of lamb stuffed with spring herbs

**SERVES 4-6**

*The herb garden really takes off again in spring. The tarragon has reappeared and the self-sown parsley is starting to germinate. I am an advocate of letting things go to seed in the garden, in the hope that the garden will regenerate itself effortlessly and this certainly happens with herbs and salad. This herb stuffed lamb is accompanied with vegetables that reflect springtime too. In this recipe I mix my small new turnips with carrots, cauliflower and peas. Ask the butcher to tunnel-bone the leg of lamb.*

1 x 2 kg (4 lb 8 oz) leg of lamb, tunnel-boned

2 garlic cloves

1 good handful each of fresh mint, parsley, oregano and thyme

6 anchovy fillets

100 g (3½ oz) bread

100 g (3½ oz) pitted green olives

1 egg

250 ml (9 fl oz) white wine

salt and pepper

**VEGETABLES**

300 g (10½ oz) turnips

300 g (10½ oz) carrots

150 g (5½ oz) shelled peas

1 small cauliflower

extra chopped parsley, mint or tarragon

a knob of butter

**TO SERVE**

steamed new potatoes

To make the stuffing, put the peeled garlic clove in a food processor and chop. Add the herbs and chop again. Add the anchovies, then the bread, roughly chopped. Process to coarse breadcrumbs.

Finally, tip in the olives and process. Season with salt and pepper to taste, remembering that the anchovies are salty. Add an egg to get everything to bind together. Make a few cuts with a sharp knife into the bone cavity of the lamb to make it a little bigger, then push the stuffing into the cavity. Pin the ends of the lamb closed with meat skewers and loosely tie up the meat with string.

Place the leg of lamb in a roasting tin. Season it well with pepper and salt and drizzle with olive oil. Place some rosemary sprigs on top. Roast at 200°C (400°F, gas 6 ) or in the middle of the Aga's roasting oven for 1½ hours. After the first half an hour baste with some wine, and continue to do this as the meat cooks.

For the vegetables, trim and quarter the turnips. Peel and cut the carrots into large chunks. Steam them until almost cooked. This can be done in advance. Cut the cauliflower into florets and add to the vegetables and steam until tender. Finally, add the peas and cook for a few extra minutes. Melt the butter, add some chopped parsley and toss the vegetables in it.

When the lamb is cooked, leave it to rest for 15 minutes before slicing. Serve it with the vegetables and the juices from the roasting dish.

# Oven-steamed brill with spinach and Dauphinoise potatoes

**SERVES 4**

*Brill is a wonderful flat fish, with delicate flesh. This is an effortless way to cook it and a complete meal in one go, especially if you cook the potatoes in the oven at the same time.*

500 g (1 lb 2 oz) spinach

2-3 cloves garlic

900 g (2 lb ) whole brill, or 4 fillets

olive oil

salt and pepper

**DRESSING**

zest and juice of a lemon

1 tbs chopped basil

1 tbs olive oil

1 tbs double cream

1 tsp Dijon mustard

**DAUPHINOISE POTATOES**

4 medium potatoes

150 ml (5½ fl oz) milk

salt and pepper

butter

Start by peeling and slicing the potatoes thinly. Butter a gratin dish and then fill with potatoes, seasoning them with salt and pepper. Heat some milk and pour on top and dot the butter around. Put the potatoes in the oven while you're preparing the fish, for approximately 20 minutes.

Bake potatoes at 200°C (400°F, gas 6) or in an Aga slide onto the middle shelf in the roasting oven.

Wash and shake dry the spinach. Line a large baking dish with silicone paper/*Bake-O-Glide* and cover with the spinach. Peel and thinly slice the garlic and scatter over the spinach.

Sprinkle with salt then lay the whole fish or the fillets on top, tucking the spinach under the fish. Season the fish with salt and pepper, drizzling a little olive oil over the fish and the spinach.

Bake in the same oven, or in an Aga, put the fish above the potato dish. Fillets will take 8-10 minutes, a whole fish may take 15-20 minutes.

For the dressing, mix everything together in a small jug.

To serve, lift the bed of spinach with the fish fillets onto warm plates. If you are serving a whole fish, serve it at the table lifting the fillets off the bone with the help of a sharp knife and a fish slice.

Accompany with the dressing in a bowl and with the Dauphinoise potatoes.

# Lemon and coriander chicken with steamed rice

SERVES 4

*This is adapted from a recipe given to me by my friend and fellow cookery teacher, Anne Jennings, who has taught several Indian cooking classes for me. The Asian flavours are quite delicate, making this a dish that can be happily served to all, straight from the pan.*

4 chicken thighs and legs

vegetable oil

5 cm (2") ginger

4 garlic cloves

½ tsp chopped chilli

½ tsp turmeric

1 tsp ground cumin seeds

1 tsp ground coriander
  seed

salt and pepper

1 lemon, zest and juice

125 ml (4½ fl oz) water

a bunch of fresh coriander

Heat a sauté pan until quite hot and then brown the chicken pieces on both sides. If you leave the skin on the meat you won't need any oil.

Peel and grate the ginger and garlic into the pan and add all the other seasonings, except the fresh coriander. Stir for a minute or so. Add the water, lemon juice and zest.

Bring to the boil, cover with a lid and simmer for 25 minutes, until the chicken is tender. In an Aga you can place it on the bottom shelf in the roasting oven until the meat is tender.

Stir in chopped coriander and serve with steamed rice.

# Steamed rice

SERVES 4-6

1 cup (225 g / 8 oz) long
  grain rice e.g.Thai
  fragrant or Basmati

1½ cups water

Put the rice in a sieve under a cold tap for a few minutes before putting it in a medium sized, thick-based saucepan, such as a cast iron one. Measure the water and pour on top. It is important that both ingredients are measured by volume. Use the same cup or mug to measure both the rice and the water, in order to get the proportions right and for perfectly cooked rice.

Bring the water and rice to a simmer. Stir well, cover with a lid and turn the heat down to the lowest possible setting. Do not uncover for 10 minutes. Turn off the heat, lift the lid and cover with a folded clean tea towel. Put the lid on top and leave for 10 minutes. The tea towel will help absorb the steam in the pot and facilitate its cooking further. When ready to serve, fork up the grains of rice with a carving fork.

# Rhubarb and honey jellies with honey madeleines

**SERVES 6+**

*Many people look forward to the rhubarb season, and there are many ways to use the delicate pink forced rhubarb in a spring dessert. Curiously, jellies have become adult desserts these days. They are light and fruity, and make a good ending to a meal.*

600 g (1lb 5 oz) pink rhubarb

water

1½ tbs clear honey

1 tbs powdered gelatine

Wash, trim and cut the rhubarb into short lengths. Put it in a saucepan with just enough water to cover. With a lid on the pan, cook for 15 minutes until very soft and juicy. Strain through a sieve into a bowl. Measure the juice – it should be about 450 ml (16 fl oz). If it isn't enough, add a little water. Stir in the honey and leave to dissolve.

Soak the gelatine in a cup with ¼ cup of cold water. When softened, melt it over a pan of hot water before stirring it into the warm juice. When the gelatine has dissolved, pour the jelly into glasses or damp jelly moulds and refrigerate to set.

If you want to turn the jellies out of their moulds, dip their bases in a bowl of hot water. Dampen the plate with the tiniest bit of water, place the plate over the jelly mould and invert quickly. Lift off the mould and slide the jelly into the middle of the plate. Wipe the plate dry if there is any water on it. Serve as it is or with a little clotted cream, and the madeleines.

# Honey madeleines

**MAKES 12-15**

1 egg

40 g (1½ oz) caster sugar

1½ tsp light brown sugar

40 g (1½ oz) plain flour

½ tsp baking powder

40 g (1½ oz) cooled melted butter

2 tsp runny honey

Put the egg and both sugars in a mixing bowl. Whisk with an electric beater until light, fluffy and voluminous.

Sift the flour and baking powder together, then sieve and fold it into the egg mixture. Finally, pour in the butter and honey, folding everything together.

Brush the *madeleine* moulds generously with butter. Using a dessert spoon, spoon the cake mixture into the moulds. Don't over fill them. If you don't have enough tins to do one baking, after one batch, wash up the moulds, dry well and re-grease.

Bake at 220°C (425°F, gas 8) or in the middle of the Aga's roasting oven, for 5-10 minutes until risen and golden. Cool for a few minutes before inverting onto a cooling rack.

# Overnight coffee cake

**SERVES 8+**

*This couldn't be easier, just take the uncooked cake from the fridge and put it in the oven in the morning in time for coffee. This recipe belongs to the great era of American hospitality, when there was always a percolating coffee pot on the go in every kitchen and some cake to go with it. So there isn't coffee in the cake – you serve coffee with the cake!*

300 g (10½ oz) plain flour

200 g (7 oz) caster sugar

100 g (3½ oz) light brown
    sugar

1 tsp bicarbonate of soda

1 tsp baking powder

½ tsp salt

1 tsp cinnamon

1 x 300 ml (10 fl oz) carton
    of buttermilk

150 g (5½ oz) cool melted
    butter

2 eggs

**TOPPING**

100 g (3½ oz) brown sugar

50g (1¾ oz) chopped
    walnuts or pecans

1 tsp cinnamon

Mix all the dry ingredients together in a bowl then add the buttermilk, melted butter and eggs. Beat together for 3 minutes with a spoon.

Spoon the mixture into a greased 26 cm (10") cake tin. Mix the topping ingredients together and sprinkle over the batter. Cover the cake with cling film and refrigerate overnight.

In the morning, uncover the cake and bake at 180°C (350°F, gas 4) for 45 minutes. In an Aga bake on the lowest shelf of the roasting oven. Test with a skewer to see that the cake is cooked. The skewer should come out clean after inserting it in the centre of the cake.

Serve the cake warm.

**NOTE**

Buttermilk can be bought at health food shops and at some supermarkets. If you can't find it, mix half the quantity of live natural yoghurt with the same amount of milk to make up the desired quantity.

# Sponge flan with fruit

SERVES 4+

*I know you can buy these sponge bases in the supermarkets but, if you make it yourself, the cake is softer and, of course, nicer. It is unbelievably quick and simple to prepare and you can cover the top with any fruit you like; strawberries in spring, cherries in summer and so on. Use a sponge flan tin with a raised edge.*

1 large egg

50 g (1¾ oz) soft (minimum 70% fat) margarine e.g. *Stork Baking*

50 g (1¾ oz) caster sugar

50 g (1¾ oz) self-raising flour

½ tsp baking powder

½ tsp vanilla extract

**TOPPING**

100 ml (3½ fl oz) natural yoghurt

100 ml (3½ fl oz) whipping cream

2 tsp honey

400 g (14 oz) fresh fruit e.g. strawberries

icing sugar

Melt a knob of butter and let it cool a little before using it to grease well a 20 cm (8") sponge flan tin. Brush the butter on thickly, making sure the fluted sides are well greased. Line the bottom of the tin with a circle of baking paper that just fits the flat centre base. This should ensure you can release the cooked cake easily from the tin.

Put all the ingredients for the sponge in a bowl and whisk until smooth and creamy using an electric mixer. Pour into the prepared tin and smooth over. Bake at 180°C (350°F, gas 4) or the bottom shelf of the Aga's roasting oven for 15-20 minutes, until puffed up, golden, firm and coming away from the sides of the tin. Cool slightly before turning out of the tin onto a serving dish with the indentation uppermost.

To make the filling, whip the cream and fold in the yoghurt and honey. Spread the mixture into the dip in the sponge. Halve or slice the fruit and arrange it to cover the cream. Sprinkle with icing sugar and serve.

# Bavarois with fresh strawberries

**SERVES 8**

*This is my favourite way to dress up strawberries in May – a bit more sophisticated than just strawberries and cream. The real vanilla flavour is the key to this delicate mousse. Adding a little cornflour to the custard base takes the worry out of boiling or not boiling a non-flour custard and the fear of a curdled mix.*

2 egg yolks

1 tsp cornflour

125 g (4½ oz) caster sugar

150 ml (5 fl oz) milk

400 ml (14 fl oz) double cream

2 level tsp powdered gelatine

1 vanilla pod

1 punnet of strawberries

sugar to taste

lemon juice to taste

Put the milk into a saucepan with the vanilla pod, sliced in half lengthways, adding half the sugar. Heat to scalding point and then remove from the heat. Cover and leave to infuse for 10 minutes.

Beat the egg yolks, cornflour and remaining sugar together in a bowl until the mixture whitens and thickens. Strain the milk onto the egg mixture, whisking it together. Scrape the seeds from the vanilla pod into the mixture.

Return the mixture to a clean saucepan and cook gently over a low heat until it thickens and comes to the boil. Pour this custard into a metal bowl to cool.

Soak the gelatine in a quarter of a cup of cold water. When it has swollen and absorbed the liquid, beat it into the hot custard. Put the custard mixture in the bowl over a larger bowl of iced water to cool and thicken. Stir in the edges as this starts to happen.

Whip the cream until just firm and put it in the fridge. Once the custard is starting to set and you can see the bottom of the custard bowl as you stir it, remove the bowl from the iced water and fold the cream into the setting custard. Pour the mixture into wetted individual moulds, or one large serving dish, and refrigerate for at least 6 hours until set.

Clean and hull the strawberries. Purée half of them with sugar and add lemon juice to taste. Halve the remaining strawberries and reserve.

To serve, warm a knife under hot water and run it round each bavarois. Briefly dip their bases in a bowl of hot water and then invert onto individual serving plates. Pour a little sauce around and garnish with the strawberries. Or serve large spoonfuls of *bavarois* from the serving dish.

# Cannoli with citrus fruits

MAKES 16

*These pastry 'pipes' filled with sweetened Ricotta cheese, are found in all the best pastry shops in Sicily. I serve* cannoli *with a fruit compote to counterbalance their richness or cut them in half to serve with coffee. It is hard to make a smaller quantity – this mixture goes a long way! Store unfilled 'pipes' in a tin.*

125 g (4½ oz) plain flour

1 tbs caster sugar

25 g (1 oz) butter

½ an egg

50 ml (1¾ fl oz) white wine

**FOR COOKING**

500 ml (18 fl oz) lard and
    sunflower oil mixed

**FILLING**

500 g (1lb 2 oz) ricotta
    cheese

icing sugar

1-2 tbs orange flower water

100 g (3½ oz) of dried
    mixed peel

**TO SERVE**

fruit salad of orange and
    grapefruit

For the dough, mix the flour and sugar in a bowl. Cut the butter into small pieces and rub it into the flour until the particles are very fine. Add the egg and wine gradually until you have a thick dough. Knead on a floured surface for five minutes. Wrap and chill the dough for 1 hour.

You can use a processor to mix in the butter and liquids and then continue mixing to knead the dough for a few minutes.

For the filling, beat the ricotta and icing sugar together adding orange flower water to taste. Stir in the dried fruit and chill until ready to use.

Cut the dough into 16 equal portions and roll each thinly into a 12.5 cm (5") circle. This can also be done with a pasta machine, stopping on the second to last setting. Wrap each circle, not too tightly, around a metal cylinder (or a piece of thick bamboo). Press gently in the middle of the tube to seal each cannoli.

Heat the lard and oil in a deep sided pan or wok. When hot but not smoking, fry the *cannoli*, a few at a time, until they are light brown (about 1½-2 minutes), turning them using tongs. Drain them on a cooling rack. When they are cool, carefully slide out the cylinders.

For the fruit salad, peel and slice up 2-3 oranges and 1 grapefruit.

When ready to serve, pipe the filling into the *cannoli*. Dust them with icing sugar and serve accompanied with a little fruit salad.

# Fresh fruit with white chocolate sauce

SERVES 4

*This is essentially an* assemblage *of ingredients accompanied by a great sauce. In early spring you won't find a lot of new season local fruit so perhaps this is the time to indulge in some of the exotic fruit from far away.*

**BISCUIT BASE**

125 g (4½ oz) soft butter

50 g (1¾ oz) caster sugar

125 g (4½ oz) plain flour

50 g (1¾ oz) rice flour

**FRUIT**

500 g (1lb 2oz) of fruit e.g. mango, kiwi, passion fruit or pineapple, orange and grapefruit

**SAUCE**

100 g (3½ oz) white chocolate

100 ml (3½ fl oz) tinned coconut milk

**TO SERVE**

a small tub of raspberry sorbet

Make the base by beating the butter and sugar together with an electric mixer until thick and fluffy. Beat in the flours. Using your hands, push the mixture into a 15 x 20 cm (6" x 8") baking tin. Bake at 180°C (350°F, gas 4), for 10-15 minutes. In an Aga, place on the shelf on the floor of the roasting oven with the heat shield above.

Cool the base and then cut into four 7 cm (3") triangles. The remaining biscuits can be cut up and stored for another occasion, or to eat with a cup of tea.

Peel and cut the fruit into thick slices.

For the sauce, gently melt the white chocolate in the coconut milk in a small saucepan.

To serve, place a biscuit base on a plate. Pile on some fruit and top with a small scoop of sorbet. Drizzle around the sauce and serve.

# Triple chocolate cake
## SERVES 8

*When Easter comes in early spring, many of us, no matter what age, start to think of chocolate. This recipe is my son Felix's contribution. He not only loves this recipe, he is very good at making it – usually to give away as a present to say thank you. There have been many lucky recipients, his guitar teacher perhaps being the first to sample it.*

*It is a simple sponge with a relatively simple filling, if you can overlook the 375 g of chocolate! Use good quality chocolate, I like* Green and Blacks*, as it 'behaves' well, when melting and mixing.*

4 eggs

100 g (3½ oz) caster sugar

75 g (2¾ oz) self-raising flour

25 g (1 oz) cocoa

**FILLING**

100 g (3½ oz) dark chocolate

100 g (3½ oz) white chocolate

450ml (15 fl oz) whipping cream

**SYRUP**

75 ml (2¾ fl oz)  water

2 tbs liqueur, e.g. brandy

1 tbs honey

**ICING**

150 g (5½ oz) milk chocolate

50 ml (1¾ fl oz) whipping cream

1 tbs unsalted butter

1-2 tbs milk

To make the sponge, whisk the eggs and sugar until really thick using an electric mixer. Sieve the flour and cocoa together into the egg mixture and fold them in carefully. Pour into a prepared (buttered and shaken with sugar) 23 cm (9") spring-form tin.

Bake at 180°C (350°F, gas 4) for 20-25 minutes. In an Aga, cook on the lowest shelf of the roasting oven with the cold shelf above. It is cooked when the cake has risen, is firm to touch and coming away from the sides of the tin. Cool the cake for a few minutes before turning it out onto a cooling rack.

To make the fillings, break up the dark and white chocolates and melt them in two separate bowls in the turned off, but still 'warmish' oven. Add a couple of spoons of cream to the white chocolate. Stir the melting chocolate from time to time. Lightly whip the cream. Cool the chocolates slightly – but don't let them get too cold. Divide the cream between the two bowls of chocolate and fold in.

To make the syrup, put the water, brandy and honey into a small saucepan and bring to the boil. Slice the cold cake into 3 thin layers. Use a long bread knife to do this. Push the point of the knife into the middle of the cake about a third of the way down the side of the cake. Use a sawing motion to cut around the cake leaving the point of the knife in the centre. Lift the top layer off and then repeat, cutting the remaining two thirds of the cake into two layers. Put the bottom layer of the cake back onto the tin's base. Spoon half the syrup over the base.

Spread the dark chocolate mix over the base cake layer. Add the second cake layer, spoon over some syrup and spread over the white chocolate mix. Place the third layer of cake on top and spoon over the remaining syrup. Each layer of cream and cake will be about equal volume. Chill until firm.

For the icing, gently melt the milk chocolate, cream and butter in a saucepan, stirring until smooth. Add a little milk to make a smooth, spreadable icing. Spread over the top and sides of the cake, using a palette knife. Refrigerate until ready to serve.

If you are serving this cake at Easter you could decorate the top of the cake with Easter eggs and little chicks.

# Summer

## Starters

## Main courses

## Desserts

# Parsley soup
**SERVES 4**

*The colour of this lovely deep green soup is due to the large amount of parsley leaves blended into the cooked soup. The other underlying flavours of this delicate soup are the parsley stalks, the celery and fennel seeds. Serve as a first course at a dinner party or for lunch with good bread and cheese.*

1 onion

1 tbs fennel seeds

1 large bunch of flat leaf parsley

4 sticks of celery

1 medium potato

1-2 tbs butter

1 litre (1¾ pt) water or vegetable stock

50 ml (2 fl oz) crème fraîche

Peel and chop the onion and place in a large soup pan with the butter, fennel seeds, parsley stalks and washed, chopped celery. Stir over a gentle heat for 10 minutes to soften the vegetables without colouring them and to bring out the flavour.

Peel and chop the potato and add to the pan along with the stock or water. Season and simmer for 10 minutes or until tender. Cool slightly before blending with the parsley leaves.

Stir in the cream and check the seasoning. Thin the soup down, if needed, with extra water or stock.

Serve the soup warm or, on a really hot day, chilled with a spoonful of yoghurt.

# Olive and tomato bread

**MAKES 1 LARGE LOAF**

*I love making bread and encouraging others to do the same. It's all about practice! Nothing to be afraid of and it will always taste better than the average shop-bought loaf. With olives and sun dried tomatoes, it can't help but be delicious and full of flavour.*

1 sachet (7 g / ¼ oz / 2 tsp) fast action dried yeast

500 g (1 lb 2 oz) strong white flour

1 tsp sea salt

350 ml (12 fl oz) hand warm water

50 g (1¾ oz) sun dried tomatoes, finely chopped

75 ml (2¾ fl oz) oil (from the tomatoes)

**FILLING**

50 g (1¾ oz) green olives, sliced

50 g (1¾ oz) black olives, sliced

2 spring onions, chopped

2 tsp thyme leaves

Mix the flour, salt and yeast together in a bowl. Stir in the chopped tomatoes. Add the olive oil to the water and pour it into the flour, mixing it to a soft dough.

Turn the dough onto a floured surface and knead for 5-10 minutes, until elastic and smooth. Alternatively you could use a mixer with a dough hook. Put the dough back into the bowl, cover with cling film and leave in a warm place for 1 hour or so until the dough has doubled in volume.

Mix the olives, spring onions and thyme together in a bowl.

Gently turn the dough onto a floured surface and push it into a large rectangle. Sprinkle over the olive filling and roll the dough up like a Swiss roll. Place the roll on a baking tray, seam side underneath and then make thick slices, without cutting all the way through. Pull each slice alternately to the left and right, exposing the open slices.

Leave the loaf to prove, for approximately an hour, until doubled in size. Bake at 200°C (400°F, gas 6) for 25-30 minutes. In an Aga, bake in the middle of the roasting oven. Serve warm or at room temperature for lunch or on a picnic.

**NOTE**

After rolling up the dough you could cut it in two and have smaller loaves; one to eat and one for the freezer.

**GETTING AHEAD**

You can always let bread rise slowly in the fridge, both for the first fermentation or the shaped loaf. This can give you some flexibility.

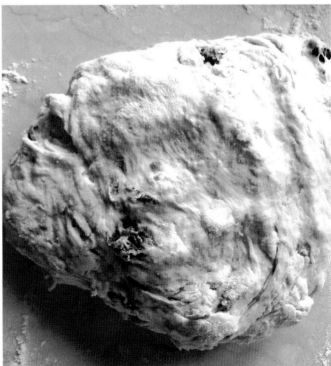

# Celery salad with white pepper zabaione
## SERVES 4-6

*This salad is so simple and light, using just a few ingredients. The secret is that everything is cut into the thinnest julienne and tossed together at the last minute with the quickly made, peppery zabaione. Its origins are from Umbria, where I run cookery weeks with Italian chef, Antonio Petruzzi.*

3 sticks celery

3-4 slices prosciutto

75 g (2¾ oz) sliced
  Emmenthal type cheese

1 tbs chopped parsley

**ZABAIONE**

2 egg yolks

2 tbs white wine

¼-½ tsp white pepper

a little salt

Wash the celery and then using a broad vegetable peeler, peel and discard the celery strings. Cut fine slices along the length of the celery using the vegetable peeler. Stack these slices and cut into 5 cm / 2" lengths. With a sharp knife, cut each stack into fine julienne (matchsticks). Place in a bowl of iced water and refrigerate until the celery is crisp.

Cut the slices of prosciutto and cheese into similar sized julienne.

When you are ready to serve the salad, drain the celery and spin it dry. Toss the three ingredients together in a bowl using your hands, adding the chopped parsley.

Make the zabaione by putting the egg yolks and wine in a large heat-proof bowl. Beat them with a balloon whisk over the gentlest heat, a very low flame. Don't let the bottom of the bowl get hotter than hand-hot. Whisk vigorously to obtain a fluffy texture. Season with lots of white pepper and a little salt.

Pour the zabaione over the salad and toss.

Serve in piles on individual plates garnished with a little extra parsley.

# Harissa eggs with roast pepper salad

**SERVES 4**

*When I worked in Venice, my employer, a Baronessa, loved any and every egg dish I served, so I have quite a large répertoire. Stuffed eggs have gone in and out of fashion over the years, so I am making a stand for the side of 'in fashion'. These eggs are soft, not dry, and if served with this modern salad they make a good first course in the summer or a filling supper or lunch dish.*

2 red and 2 yellow peppers

2 cloves of garlic, crushed

400 g (14 oz) ripe vine
  tomatoes

a little sugar

4 tbs olive oil

**CROUTONS**

1 thick slice of bread

1 tsp each of olive oil and
  butter

4 hard boiled eggs

1 tbs crème fraîche

1 tbs mayonnaise

2 tsp harissa

salt and pepper

**TO SERVE**

200 g (7 oz) washed rocket
  or other salad leaves

extra virgin olive oil

Halve and de-seed the peppers then thickly slice them. Also thickly slice the tomatoes. Place the vegetables on a baking tray, crush the garlic over the top and sprinkle a little sugar on the tomato slices. Roast for 20-30 minutes until soft, at 400°C (200°F, gas 6) or in the middle of the Aga's roasting oven. Remove from the oven and allow to cool.

To make the croutons, cube a thick slice of bread and place on a baking tray with a teaspoon each of oil and butter. Place in the oven at the same time as the tomatoes. Bake until golden – about 5-8 minutes, shaking the tray occasionally.

Halve the hard boiled eggs and scoop out the yolks. Crush them with a fork in a bowl. Add the crème fraîche, mayonnaise and harissa. Mix everything together and check the seasoning. Fill the egg whites, piling the filling into the hollows. Refrigerate until firm – about 30 minutes.

To serve, toss the salad leaves with a little extra virgin olive oil. Divide between four plates and spoon over the peppers and tomatoes. Add egg halves and scatter over the croutons.

**NOTE**

To make your own harissa, finely chop 1 fresh red chilli and 1-2 garlic cloves. Stir in 1 teaspoon each of ground caraway seeds and cumin seeds. Then mix in 1 teaspoon each of tomato purée, vinegar and paprika. Finally, stir in 2 tablespoons of olive oil. Season with salt and pepper. Any leftovers will keep in a jar in the fridge for several weeks.

**GETTING AHEAD**

Filling eggs and baking the vegetables and croutons can be done a day ahead.

# Tomatoes with ricotta and tapenade
## SERVES 4

*The French and Italians are fond of stuffed vegetables and so am I. The natural sweetness of ricotta cheese complements the tomatoes, with the saltiness of the tapenade giving a pleasant contrast. I like to make my own tapenade and, in this case, I add a little mayonnaise to it to give it a creamy texture.*

4 large (or 8 medium) ripe tomatoes

2 tbs olive oil

1 tbs balsamic vinegar

1 cucumber

salad leaves

1 ripe avocado

200 g (7 oz) ricotta cheese

100 g (3½ oz) tapenade

### TAPENADE

100 g (3½ oz) stoned black olives

2 cloves of garlic

2-3 anchovy fillets

olive oil

1 tbs mayonnaise

pepper and salt

Cut a little cross in the top of the tomatoes and with the point of a small knife cut out the cores. Drop the tomatoes into a bowl of boiling water. After 30 seconds, when you can see the skins coming away, remove the tomatoes and immerse in cold water. Pull off the tomatoes' skins.

Slice off the tops of the tomatoes and scoop out the insides. Season with salt inside the tomatoes and invert them. Sieve the tomato seeds and mix the resulting tomato juice with the olive oil and balsamic vinegar.

With a vegetable peeler, run down the cucumber to produce long ribbons of flesh. Wash the salad leaves and peel and slice the avocado. Divide this salad mixture between plates.

Fill the tomatoes with the ricotta and place on the plates. Top the tomatoes with a generous dollop of tapenade. Pour the dressing around the salad and serve with good bread or savoury biscuits.

To make the tapenade, blend the olives, garlic and anchovy fillets together until fairly smooth. Add enough olive oil to make a paste, about 50 ml (2 fl oz). Spoon in the mayonnaise. Check the seasoning, adding pepper and perhaps a little salt.

### GETTING AHEAD
Prepare the tomatoes earlier in the day and leave upside down, unfilled, in the fridge. Make the tapenade earlier. It will keep for a week in the fridge.

# Mini kebabs of chicken and melon
## SERVES 4

*Teenagers like this dish because, apart from looking good on a plate, it is easy to make and has a delightful blend of flavours and textures.*

*They make good finger food at a party too and can be assembled ahead of time and refrigerated.*

1 large chicken breast

1 lime

pepper

¼ tsp chopped chilli (from a jar)

1 cm ginger root

sunflower oil

1 tbs crème fraîche

2 tbs lemon juice

2-3 tbs dried coconut slices

½ ripe Galia melon

1 little gem lettuce

2 spring onions

Remove the skin from the chicken, cut into 2 cm / 1" cubes and marinate in lime juice, salt, pepper, freshly grated ginger and chopped chilli, if liked, for half an hour.

Drain the chicken cubes before searing in a hot pan with a little oil. Cook for 5 minutes until brown all over and then leave to cool.

Mix the crème fraîche and lemon juice together. Peel and dice the melon into cubes about the same size as the chicken pieces.

Wash and dry the lettuce leaving the leaves whole and place them on plates.

Place a total of 3 pieces of chicken and melon on tooth picks and place 2 or 3 mini kebabs on the lettuce.

Scatter over some coconut and spoon over the dressing. Slice the spring onions, scatter on top and serve.

# Peach and Gruyère tart

**SERVES 4-8**

*This tart is surprising as it combines quite salty ingredients with the sweetness of ripe peaches. It is great party food, can be made in advance and can be served on many different occasions from buffets and picnics to smart dinner parties.*

200 g (7 oz) plain flour

100 g (3½ oz) cold butter, roughly chopped

2 tbs water

1 mozzarella cheese ball, 250 g (9 oz) drained weight

4-5 slices of prosciutto

75 g (2¾ oz) Gruyère cheese

4 good sized ripe peaches

To make the pastry, put the flour, butter and tablespoons of water in a food processor and blend until the pastry comes together in a ball.

Roll the pastry onto a paper lined baking sheet to form a 30 cm (12") square. Turn the sides up to form a little edge and pinch firmly in place.

Thinly slice the mozzarella and peaches and grate the Gruyère. First lay the mozzarella over the pastry. Cover with slices of prosciutto, then the Gruyère. Finally, place the sliced peaches on top.

Bake at 180°C (350°F, gas 4) or in the lower part of an Aga's roasting oven, for 30 minutes until golden.

Serve warm slices as a starter or with a salad as a light meal. Cut into small squares, this tart makes excellent finger food at a party.

**GETTING AHEAD**

The pastry can be made a couple of days ahead and stored in the fridge, and the tart can be assembled several hours ahead and kept in the fridge until you are ready to bake it.

# Rolled rump steak with carrots and ginger
## SERVES 4

*This is a really attractive dish – vegetables wrapped in thin beef slices marinated in a soy mixture make a delicious main course. Serve with the noodle salad.*

8 x 100 g (3½ oz) thin
  slices of rump steak

100 g (3½ oz) fresh ginger

2 carrots

1 bunch asparagus or 200 g
  (7 oz) French beans

1 yellow pepper

MARINADE

2 tbs sunflower oil

2 tbs light soy sauce

1 tsp sugar

2 garlic cloves

¼ tsp minced chilli

NOODLES

200 g (7 oz) rice noodles

50 ml (2 fl oz) fish sauce

50 ml (2 fl oz) lime juice

1 tsp caster sugar

1 red onion

100 g (3½ oz) radishes

Break off the tough ends of the asparagus and discard. If you are using beans, trim top and bottom. Peel the carrot and cut into pieces the same thickness and length as the asparagus or beans. Steam the two vegetables until half cooked – about 3-4 minutes. Peel and cut the ginger into fine julienne. Cut the yellow pepper into sticks the same width as the carrots.

Lay the slices of beef out and place 2-3 asparagus spears or beans across the meat. Add some carrot, pepper and ginger. Roll up and secure with a toothpick. Mix all the marinade ingredients and pour over the rolled rump steak. Leave to marinate for at least an hour.

To cook the meat, heat a frying pan until hot and then cook the rolls for about 5 minutes, turning as they brown.

To serve, soak the noodles in hot water for 3 minutes, then drain well. Mix with the fish sauce, lime juice and sugar. Thinly slice the red onion and radishes and toss with the noodles.

NOTE

For a vegetarian dish, use a peeler to make thin slices of courgette. Lay three slices overlapping to form a rectangle. Place the filling across the end and roll up carefully. Marinate, then fry as above.

# Chicken with prosciutto and tomato chutney
## SERVES 4

*Here is a dish that is good for entertaining as it can be prepared well in advance. Serving chutney as a sauce makes things very easy – it's the perfect accompaniment. Your own home-made chutney will give the dish that extra zing.*

3-4 chicken breasts

2 x 125 g balls of
   mozzarella cheese

4 slices of Italian dried ham

2 tsp chopped sage leaves

1 jar tomato chutney

300 g (10½ oz) broccoli

4 tbs almond flakes

1 tbs butter

fresh basil leaves

butter

**TO SERVE**

crushed potatoes

Slice the mozzarella and cover the top of the chicken with the slices. Sprinkle over the chopped herbs.

Drape the slices of ham over the chicken pieces and place them on a lightly oiled, shallow roasting dish. Place in a hot oven, 200°C (400°F, gas 6) or in the middle of the Aga's roasting oven and roast for 15 minutes.

Cut the broccoli into florets and steam until tender. Fry the slivered almonds in butter and then pour them over the vegetables.

Slice each chicken breast into 3-4 slices. Serve on warm plates accompanied with the tomato chutney and broccoli.

To make the crushed potatoes, boil or steam some new potatoes. When cooked, crush them lightly with a masher to just break them up. Season with a little olive oil, pepper and salt and stir in some chopped rocket or watercress leaves.

**GETTING AHEAD**

Assemble the chicken and place in the fridge to cook later.

# Lamb shoulder with aubergine salad and yoghurt sauce
**SERVES 4**

*Being an Australian, I never tire of lamb, despite having it served in our childhood six out of seven days a week. Warm salads were not a part of my childhood, they are a more modern invention, but on a summer's evening, serving warm roast or barbequed lamb on a bed of salad makes a very pleasing meal. We have come a long way from meat and three veg!*

2 tbs olive oil

500 g (1 lb 2 oz) boned half
   shoulder of lamb

SAUCE

200 ml (7 fl oz) Greek yoghurt

½ tsp chilli paste

2 tbs chopped mint

SALAD

5 small raw beetroot

1 large aubergine

2 tbs olive oil

1 crisp lettuce

1 bunch of radishes

1 bunch or white small
   salad onions

1 sprig each of rosemary
   and thyme, chopped

Slice the aubergine thinly and grill both sides until just starting to colour. You don't need any oil for this, but when they are cooked, toss in a bowl with a little olive oil and season with pepper and salt.

Peel the beetroot and cut into small wedges. Toss in 1-2 teaspoons of oil. Season with salt and pepper and pour into a small roasting dish. Bake at 180°C, (350°F, gas 4) or in the middle of the Aga's roasting oven, covered with foil until tender, approximately 10 minutes.

Thinly slice the radishes. Peel and thinly slice the onions. Combine in a bowl, cover with water and refrigerate to crisp up.

Place the lamb in a small roasting pan and roast for 15-20 minutes. Cook at 200°C (400°F, gas 6) or above the centre in an Aga's roasting oven. Test that the meat is cooked with the point of a sharp knife. If the juices are light pink the meat will be rosy. If the juices are clear, the meat will be well done.

If you would rather barbeque the meat, place it over a hot barbeque and turn it as it cooks, for about 15-20 minutes. Leave the meat to rest away from the heat for 5 minutes.

Make the sauce by mixing the yoghurt, chilli paste and the chopped mint.

To serve, drain the radishes and onions and toss all the prepared vegetables together with the chopped rosemary and thyme and the remaining olive oil. Season to taste.

Wash and dry the lettuce. Slice the lamb thickly. Cover a platter with lettuce and all the vegetables. Place the sliced lamb on top and accompany with a bowl of sauce.

# Crispy duck salad with red fruits

**SERVES 4**

*I love serving this dish with all the soft red fruits of summer. It makes an elegant first course or a stunning main dish on a hot day.*

1 x 1 kg (2 lb 4 oz) duck meat (breast or legs)

1 onion, chopped

1 large carrot, chopped

2 sticks celery, chopped

1 red oak leaf lettuce

200 g (7 oz) red cherries

100 g (3½ oz) raspberries

50 g (1¾ oz) redcurrants

50 g (1¾ oz) blackcurrants

1 bunch of chives

**DRESSING**

100 g (3½ oz) fresh raspberries

1 tsp brown sugar

2 tbs red wine vinegar

1 garlic clove, crushed

½ tsp Dijon mustard

50 ml (2 fl oz) sunflower oil

To cook the duck, season with salt and pepper and place in a roasting dish, on a bed of the chopped root vegetables. Cover with foil.

Roast at 180°C (350°F, gas 4) for one hour. In an Aga cook in the roasting oven on the lowest shelf.

Make the dressing by mixing the raspberries, sugar, vinegar, garlic and mustard together. Mash raspberries to a pulp and press everything through a sieve. Gradually whisk the oil into the strained raspberry juice and season with salt and pepper.

Wash and dry the salad, and tear into pieces. Pit the cherries and remove the currants from their stalks.

Strip the skin from the cooked duck. Grill it until crisp then snip it into strips. Remove the meat from the bone and then shred the meat with your fingers or a knife.

To serve, arrange the salad leaves on plates and scatter over the shredded duck and the fruit. Pour over the dressing. Top with the crispy skin and chopped fresh chives.

**GETTING AHEAD**

You can cook and shred the duck the day before. Also make the dressing a day ahead.

# Home-made pappardelle with courgettes and lemon
SERVES 4-8

*If you have a pasta machine, try this simple recipe. It is important to use pasta flour which is easy to find these days.*

2 x 60 g (2 oz) eggs

200 g (7 oz) pasta flour or Italian type 00 flour

## SAUCE

750 g (1 lb 10 oz) courgettes

100 g (3½ oz) butter

1 lemon

2 tsp wine vinegar

50 g (1¾ oz) pistachios

1 packet 25 g (1 oz) fresh basil

To make the pasta dough, put the flour in a mound on the kitchen bench. Make a well in the middle and crack in the eggs. Using a fork, stir the flour into the eggs until as much as possible has been absorbed. Mix with your hands until a smooth paste is reached.

Knead the dough with the heel of your hand for 5 minutes until the dough is smooth and velvety. Test by pushing a finger into the centre – the dough should be elastic and dry in the middle.

Alternatively, put the flour and eggs in a food processor or bowl of an electric mixer and blend until it all comes together. If a little dry, add water a teaspoon at a time until you can bring the dough together with your hands.

Wrap the dough in cling film and let it rest for 15 minutes or more, before rolling it out.

Cut the dough in two, and rewrap the other piece. Roll the dough through the pasta machine on its widest setting. Fold it in half and repeat 5-6 times until the pasta has a velvety texture.

Gradually reduce the machine setting, rolling the pasta through each decreasing setting to make the pasta sheet thinner. Stop rolling through at the second to last setting. Cut the sheet of pasta into 30 cm / 12" pieces and lay them on a floured tea towel or hang on a pasta rack to dry a little. Repeat the whole process with the other piece of dough. To cut the pappardelle, use a pastry wheel to cut 2 cm (1") wide strips about 30 cm (12") long.

To make the sauce, slice the courgettes very thinly lengthways using a potato peeler. Heat the butter in a saucepan until frothy, then stir in the lemon rind, cut in fine julienne, the lemon juice and the chopped pistachios. Add the vinegar, and chopped basil.

Cook the pappardelle in a large pot of boiling salted water for about 4 minutes, adding the courgettes in the last minute. Drain immediately and pour into a big bowl. Pour over the sauce, toss gently and serve.

# Summer lasagne

## SERVES 4

*There are many evenings in an English summer when we wish it was hot enough to be eating outdoors. However, on cooler evenings, when we have to retreat to the kitchen, this summer lasagne is perfect. Now you know how to make fresh pasta, here is another recipe to use.*

150 g (5½ oz) fresh lasagne sheets made with 1 egg + 100 g (3½ oz) flour

200 g (7 oz) fresh spinach

250 g (9 oz) ricotta cheese

100 g (3½ oz) smoked bacon or salami

25 g (1 oz) grated Parmesan

### SAUCE

1 onion

2 garlic cloves

2 tbs olive oil

500 g (1 lb 2 oz) mince pork or beef

150 ml (5 fl oz) white wine

1 x 400 g tin chopped tomatoes

2 tbs chopped fresh oregano

salt and pepper

First make the sauce. Chop the onion and garlic and cook in a sauté pan until they soften. Add the minced pork, turning up the heat, and fry to break up the meat. Now add the wine and let it almost evaporate before adding the tomatoes and herbs. Season well with pepper and salt and simmer for 30 minutes.

Wash the spinach and cook it in a sauté pan with just the water clinging to the leaves, until it wilts. Drain and roughly chop. Slice up the bacon or salami into bits. Cook the lasagne in boiling salted water until *al dente*. Drain and leave in a bowl of cold water until ready to use.

To assemble the lasagne, spoon a little sauce onto the bottom of a 20 x 30 cm / 8" x 12" oven-to-tableware lasagne dish. Drain the cooked pasta sheets. Scatter a little meat sauce over the base of the dish and then cover with a layer of pasta. Spoon over a good layer of meat sauce, then add another layer of pasta. Dot around teaspoonfuls of spinach and ricotta cheese plus a sprinkling of bacon. Repeat the layers finishing with a top layer of spinach, ricotta and bacon. You will probably have four pasta layers depending on the size of your dish. Dust with Parmesan cheese.

Bake at 200°C (400°F, gas 6) for 20 minutes. In an Aga, place in the middle of the roasting oven for 20 minutes. Leave to settle for 10 minutes before serving warm.

### GETTING AHEAD

Make the lasagne up to a day ahead and refrigerate until ready to cook.

# Sweet and sour halibut with herb and chilli salad
## SERVES 4

*The beautiful creamy white meat of halibut is very seductive. The flavour is delicate yet it stands up well to the accompanying Thai salad. Serve on a summer's day as a main course.*

4 halibut steaks

1-2 tsb olive oil

1 fresh red chilli

1 small bunch fresh
   coriander leaves

1 small bunch of mint
   leaves

4 shallots

100 g (3½ oz) mange-tout
   peas

DRESSING

2 tsp brown sugar

2 tsp granulated sugar

4 tbs water

2 tbs fish sauce

4 tbs lime juice

GARNISH

lime wedges

Slice the chilli thinly, discarding the seeds. Peel and finely slice the shallots. Top and tail the peas, blanch, drain and refresh under cold water and then thinly slice lengthways. Tear up the mint and coriander leaves. Mix with the chilli, shallot and pea slices.

To make the dressing, put the sugars and water in a small saucepan along with the fish sauce and lime juice. Swirl the pan over a medium heat until combined and heated through. Cool and then mix with the herb salad.

Season the fish with salt and toss in 1 tablespoon of olive oil. Heat a frying pan over medium heat, adding a little more oil. When it is hot, add the fish. When the fish is starting to brown – after 2 minutes – turn it over and cook the other side. The fish is done when the flesh is opaque and white. Press a small knife into the flesh to see that it is cooked through.

Serve the fish on warm plates with a spoonful of salad on top, accompanied with lime wedges.

GETTING AHEAD

Make the salad ahead and refrigerate. Also make the dressing, but combine the two only when ready to serve.

# Meringue baskets with summer berries

**SERVES 4+**

*The black and redcurrants are ripening in June and the garden paths are overflowing with little wild strawberries, mostly self-sown. What better way to serve them than in a soft meringue basket? Even if you have only a little space I would encourage you to have a couple of fruit bushes. They can be in amongst the flower beds or in large containers. If you have the fruit, you can really indulge in these delicious puddings.*

2 egg whites (50 ml / 2 fl oz)

pinch each cream of tartar and salt

100 g (3½ oz) caster sugar

¾ tsp cornflour

¾ tsp vinegar

200 ml (7 fl oz) whipping cream

300 g (10½ oz) redcurrants, blackcurrants or raspberries

50 g (1¾ oz) caster sugar

½ tsp cinnamon

**GARNISH**

extra berries

Beat the whites with the salt and cream of tartar until they form soft peaks. Beat in half the sugar, a spoonful at a time, until the whites are stiff. Mix the rest of the sugar and cornflour together and whisk into the meringues. Finally, whisk in the vinegar.

Liberally paint small tart tins, or Yorkshire pudding tins, with melted butter and dust each with flour, shaking out any excess. Spoon the meringue into the tins, making indentations in the centres. Bake at 140°C (275°F, gas 1) for 30-40 minutes (depending on your oven) until the meringues set. In an Aga, place the meringues in the simmering oven. They will take a little longer to cook. Leave the meringues to cool in the tins.

Place the fruit in a small saucepan with a couple of tablespoons of water and cook for 1-2 minutes until the berries start to collapse a little. Sweeten with sugar and a little ground cinnamon to taste. Purée in a blender. Sieve the fruit to remove the seeds, if you wish.

To serve, remove the meringue from the tins. Place on plates and top with cooked fruit. Whip the cream and add a dollop on top of each pudding. Garnish with more berries.

**GETTING AHEAD**

Make the meringues one or two days ahead, leaving them in the tins. The purée can be made days ahead too. Whip the cream lightly a couple of hours before you are ready to use it and keep refrigerated.

**VARIATIONS**

Try lemon curd in the winter instead of summer fruit purées.

# Buttered plum tarts with raspberries
## SERVES 8+

*When the Victoria plums appear I like to make these tartlets. The fruit needs very little cooking, just a little heating through in a hot buttery pan. Don't let the fruit get too soft. The butter and sugar plum juice make a lovely syrupy sauce. After you fill the tarts, heat the raspberries through in the same pan – just for a minute and then add to the top of the tart. The whole thing will look like a sparkling delicious jewel.*

### SWEET PASTRY

175 g (6 oz) plain flour

100 g (3½ oz) butter

2 tbs caster sugar

1 egg

750 g (1 lb 10 oz) Victoria plums

1 cup raspberries

50 g (3½ oz) butter

1-2 tbs golden caster sugar

Make the pastry by blending the flour and butter together in a food processor or by rubbing it in with your fingertips. Stir in the sugar and then the egg. Tip onto a floured work surface and draw the dough into a ball with a little gentle kneading.

Break the dough into walnut size pieces. Roll each one out to fit the tartlet moulds, cutting neat edges with a knife or 10 cm / 4" biscuit cutter. Freeze the pastry shells until cold and set.

Bake blind (see note below) in a preheated oven at 180°C (350°F, gas 4), or in the lower half of the Aga's roasting oven until light golden, about 8-10 minutes.

Halve or quarter plums and place in a saucepan with the butter and sugar. When ready to serve the tarts, place the pan on the heat. Gently stir the plums just until the sugar and butter has melted and the fruit is warm.

Pour the plums into the tartlets. Heat the raspberries for a minute in the same pan and pour over the plums. Serve straightaway with some cream in a jug.

### NOTE

This is the perfect sweet tart base – a bit biscuity, thin and crunchy, so only fill them when you are about to serve the tartlets. I use *Silverwood's* Yorkshire pudding trays – each indentation is the perfect size for an individual portion. If you have a second tray place it on top to bake the pastry blind – far less fiddly than paper and weights or dry beans. The top tray keeps the pastry in place and the heat transmitted through it helps cook the pastry. Uncooked pastry lined trays can be kept in the freezer and cooked straight from frozen. Cooked empty tartlet shells will keep well in an airtight cake tin.

# Tartlets with melon, kiwi fruit and mango purée
## SERVES 4

*Now you've mastered the pastry, here is another filling – mango, kiwi and melon – that you might like to try.*

4 cooked tartlet shells

**FILLING**

1 ripe mango

½ ripe melon

2 kiwi fruit

Peel the mango and cut the fruit away from the stone. Purée in a food processor. Spread the mango purée on the bottom of the cooked tartlet shells.

Peel the kiwi fruit and slice up. Cut the melon in half and discard the seeds. Make some melon balls using a melon baller (Parisian scoop).

Cover the tartlets with sliced kiwi fruit and melon balls. Decorate with a mint leaf and serve.

**GETTING AHEAD**

Make the mango purée earlier in the day. Cover with clingfilm and refrigerate. The melon balls and sliced kiwi can also wait in the fridge. Assemble only when ready to eat otherwise the pastry will go soggy.

# Peaches in Prosecco, semolina squares & hazelnut ice-cream

**SERVES 4**

*Ripe peaches are sublime so I think they should be served as simply as possible. However, I have included two recipes here that make great accompaniments: semolina squares and hazelnut ice-cream. You could serve one or both to go with the peaches.*

4 large ripe peaches

2-3 tbs caster sugar

300 ml (½ pt) Prosecco

Peel the peaches by soaking them in a bowl of boiling water. Leave for one minute then try to pull the peel off with your fingertips. If it comes off easily, pour off the boiling water and cover the peaches with cold water whilst you peel all the fruit.

Put the peaches in a bowl with the sugar and the Prosecco. Leave to marinate in the fridge for several hours.

To serve, place the peaches in bowls and pour over some of the marinade. Accompany with the semolina squares and / or the hazelnut ice-cream.

# Semolina squares

**MAKES 12**

100 g (3½ oz) melted butter

125 g (4½ oz) caster sugar

175 g (6 oz) fine semolina

¾ tsp baking powder

1 tsp vanilla

75 ml (2¾ fl oz) natural
    yoghurt

25 g (1 oz) slivered almonds

**SYRUP**

100 ml (3½ fl oz) water

200 g (7 oz) granulated
    sugar

pared rind and juice ½ lemon
    or 1 lime

Stir everything together except for the almonds and pour into a greased 22 cm (9") square tin. Smooth over the mixture and sprinkle with slivered almonds.

Bake at 180°C (350°F, gas 4) or in the lower half of the Aga's roasting oven for 20 minutes until risen and golden.

Combine the syrup ingredients, except the lemon juice, in a saucepan and heat gently to dissolve the sugar, then simmer for 2 minutes. Add the lemon juice and spoon the syrup over the cake whilst warm. Leave the cake to cool and then cut into squares.

These pastries can be made in advance, stored in a cake tin and brought out with coffee instead of serving a dessert.

# Hazelnut ice-cream

**SERVES 8**

*You may ask why make your own ice-cream when there is so much available in the shop? My answer is home-made is always better. This one certainly is.*

500 ml (18 fl oz) natural
  yoghurt

75 g (2¾ oz) icing sugar

100 g (3½ oz) hazelnuts

Toast the hazelnuts first by putting them in a hot oven for about 5 minutes until lightly coloured. Leave to cool then rub off the skins. Roughly chop the nuts.

Mix the yoghurt with the icing sugar and toasted hazelnuts. Pour into an ice-cream machine to churn or pour into a cake tin and place in the freezer until firm.

# Cherry strudel
## SERVES 8+

*I have fond memories of the fruit strudels served in a Hungarian pastry shop at Bondi. They had so many different varieties that we would keep going back and back for visits. This café was really leading the way in tempting us Aussies to broaden our food palates. As it is easy to find filo pastry now, you can make a strudel quite effortlessly.*

50 g (1¾ oz) fresh breadcrumbs

50 g (1¾ oz) ground almonds

100 g (3½ oz) butter

1 x 250 g packet of filo pastry

**FILLING**

450 g (1 lb) cherries, stoned

250 g (9 oz) pears, peeled cored and sliced

50 g (1¾ oz) caster sugar

1 tsp cinnamon

25 g (1 oz) flaked almonds

zest ½ lemon

150 g (5½ oz) curd or cottage cheese

**TO SERVE**

icing sugar and crème fraîche

Melt the butter and use half to fry the breadcrumbs and ground almonds until golden. Set aside.

Stir all the filling ingredients together in a bowl.

Lay out some filo sheets, overlapping each to form a 26 cm (10") square. The number of sheets you need might vary from 2-4 depending on the packet. Brush the pastry square with some of the remaining butter. Continue to layer up the filo sheets, painting each layer with butter. Brush the top sheet with butter and sprinkle over the fried crumbs.

Evenly spread the filling, right up to the edges, over the filo square and roll up like a Swiss roll. Do not roll too tightly, otherwise the pastry will burst open on baking. You can cut the strudel in half to form two shorter ones if you like.

Place the strudel, seam-side down on a baking sheet. Brush with the remaining butter and bake at 180°C (350°F, gas 4) or in the bottom of the Aga's roasting oven, for 20-25 minutes until crisp and golden.

Serve warm, cut in thick slices, with a dusting of icing sugar and with crème fraîche on the side.

**GETTING AHEAD**

Cooked strudel will keep well for several days in the fridge. It also freezes well. Reheat for 15 minutes to crisp up the pastry and serve warm.

# Redcurrant torte

**SERVES 8+**

*Living in rural England, I have masses of red and blackcurrants in my garden. This is a real contrast to my Australian cooking life. This recipe was one of Roger's favourite summer desserts. The redcurrant layer is barely cooked, so the fruit really keeps its fresh flavour.*

## BASE

75 g (2¾ oz) softened butter

50 g (1¾ oz) caster sugar

2 egg yolks

50 g (1¾ oz) ground almonds

150 g (5½ oz) self-raising flour

## FILLING

500 g (1 lb 2 oz) red currants

100 g (3½ oz) caster sugar

## MERINGUE

4 egg whites

100 g (3½ oz) caster sugar

To make the cake base, cream the butter and sugar together, then beat in the egg yolks followed by the ground almonds and self-raising flour. This can also be done in a food processor.

Grease a 23 cm (9") spring-form tin and spread the cake base over the bottom. Bake at 180°C (350°F, gas 4) for 15-20 minutes, until golden and risen. In an Aga, bake on the lowest shelf of the roasting oven.

Remove the redcurrants from their stalks, place in a bowl and stir in the sugar. Tip on top of the cake base.

Beat the egg whites until stiff and then gradually beat in the sugar until you have firm peaks. Cover the redcurrants with the meringue, making nice peaks.

Bake the finished cake immediately in a hot oven, 200°C (400°F, gas 6) for 5 minutes until golden. In an Aga, bake in the middle of the roasting oven.

Serve warm, cut in wedges with pouring cream to accompany it. It is also good served cold.

## GETTING AHEAD

Cook the base and cover with the redcurrant layer. Make the meringue layer just before cooking the torte if you want to serve it warm.

# Apricot cake
## SERVES 8

*This cake is lovely served with tea or as a dessert with lightly whipped cream. It is very quick to prepare and during July, when my apricots ripen I make it often. This year, we picked 12 kilos from a single tree. I was thrilled. What a bumper crop!*

100 g (3½ oz) butter

100 g (3½ oz) caster sugar

150 g (5½ oz) self-raising flour

1 tsp baking powder

2 eggs

50 ml (1¾ fl oz) milk

1½ tsp ground cinnamon

½ a grated nutmeg

200 g (7 oz) ripe apricots

Melt the butter without letting it get too hot.

Remove the stones from the apricots and cut the fruit into quarters.

Measure all the dry ingredients into a bowl, add eggs and pour over the melted butter. Stir until you have a smooth mixture. Finally, stir in the fruit.

Pour into a greased 20 cm (8") cake tin and bake at 180°C (350°F, gas 4) for about 40 minutes. In an Aga, bake in the lower half of the roasting oven with the heat shield above. The cake is cooked when well risen, golden and coming away from the sides of the tin. When you press the top of the cake gently, it should bounce back.

Dust with icing sugar and serve warm or cold.

# Autumn

# Tomato and pepper tart
## SERVES 8

*Autumn is a time when we are still harvesting from the garden and fields. In fact, it takes all summer for tomatoes to ripen up here in south west England, so invariably, I have more tomatoes in September than August. There is quite a bit of preparation for this dish but it is well worth the effort. I have served it cut in little squares as a canapé, and also in larger slices as a first course or supper dish.*

500 g (1 lb 2 oz) ready-made puff pastry

6 red peppers

1 kg (2 lb 4 oz) ripe tomatoes

4 cloves garlic

2 chillies or ½-1 tsp chopped chilli

1 small tin of anchovy fillets

salt and pepper

3 tbs olive oil

egg yolk to glaze

Halve and de-seed the peppers, then grill them until the skins blister and blacken. Remove from the grill and cover with cling film. When cool enough to handle, pull off the peel, and cut the peppers into thin strips.

Peel, seed and chop the tomatoes. Halve and de-seed the chilli and chop finely. Chop the garlic. Heat the oil in a sauté pan and cook the tomatoes, garlic, and chilli for 10 minutes.

Add the pepper strips and simmer for another 10 minutes. Season well, then leave to cool.

Roll out the pastry into a rectangle 45 cm (18") x 26 cm (10"). Cut away a strip 1 cm (½") wide all around the pastry. Brush the edges of the pastry rectangle and then place the cut out pastry strips around its edge to form the sides. Prick the bottom of the tart with a fork.

Glaze with egg yolk, and mark a criss-cross pattern on the top edges with the back of a small knife. Bake at 220°C (425°F, gas 7) for 20 minutes. In an Aga, cook the tart in the middle of the roasting oven. Leave to cool and gently push the centre of the pastry down if it has risen. Spoon in the filling.

Cut thin strips of anchovy and make a lattice top over the tomatoes. Bake the tart for 15 minutes.

Serve hot or cold, unaccompanied or with some salad leaves.

# Venison and fennel salad
## SERVES 6

*This dish takes me back to the cooking classes I have held in Umbria. This is a variation on a Bresaola salad, and a way to make a little venison go a long way. It makes an elegant first course.*

50 ml (2 fl oz) olive oil

juice 1 lemon

1 tsp flaked salt

2 tbs crushed peppercorns

450 g (1 lb) venison fillet
  from the haunch

2 fennel bulbs

100 g (3½ oz) Parmesan
  cheese

Mix the oil, lemon juice, salt and pepper in a bowl. Rub half of the dressing over the venison. Tie the meat at 2 cm (1") intervals, to make a firm cylindrical shape.

Heat a small oven-proof frying pan until really hot. Brown the meat on all sides for about 5 minutes. Put it into a hot oven, 200°C (400°F, gas 6) or in the middle of the Aga's roasting oven for 8-10 minutes.

Remove the meat from the oven and allow to cool. The meat should be fairly rare when cold.

Cut away any dry outer leaves of the fennel. Halve and cut out the core, then slice the fennel thinly. You can do this with a mandolin. Leave the sliced fennel to get crisp in a bowl of iced water.

To serve, thinly slice the venison and arrange on plates, covering them in a single layer. Drain and dry the fennel on kitchen paper. Pile the fennel on top of the venison and drizzle over the remaining dressing. Using a broad vegetable peeler, shave some Parmesan over the salad and serve.

## NOTE
Beef fillet can be substituted for venison.

## GETTING AHEAD
Cook the venison a day ahead and refrigerate whole. Prepare the fennel on the day, keeping it in a bowl of iced water in the fridge.

# Garden minestrone
## SERVES 6

*When I dreamed up this soup, I was thinking about how I could use up the inevitable glut of courgettes and cherry tomatoes in my garden, and basil in the greenhouse. This autumn Minestrone will help prolong memories of summers passed.*

1 clove garlic

2 sticks of celery

1 red onion

2-4 tbs olive oil

450 g (1 lb) courgettes, yellow or green

salt and pepper

1 litre (1¾ pts) vegetable stock or water

450 g (1 lb) ripe cherry tomatoes, red and yellow if you have them

2 tbs chopped marjoram and thyme

150 ml (5 fl oz) double cream

### PESTO

25  g (1 oz) fresh basil

2 tbs pine nuts

2 crushed garlic cloves

2 tbs extra virgin olive oil

1 tbs of grated Parmesan cheese

### TO SERVE

50 g (1¾ oz) grated Parmesan cheese

Finely dice the garlic, celery and onion and gently sauté them in a large soup pan in the oil for 10 minutes, without colouring them, and until they are soft.

Wash the courgettes, top and tail then dice them into 1 cm (½") pieces. Add to the soup pot and sauté, stirring to coat with the oil, for a further 10 minutes.

Add the stock to the pot and season with salt and pepper. Simmer for 20 minutes. Cool slightly before blending half the soup in a food processor, then return this to the soup pot.

Prepare the tomatoes, cutting them into quarters. In a sauté pan, heat a little more olive oil. Add the tomatoes and herbs and cook gently to thicken slightly. Season with salt and pepper, then stir into the courgette base.

To finish the soup, stir in the cream. Serve immediately in large soup plates, with a spoonful of basil pesto in the middle of each one. Accompany with a bowl of grated Parmesan cheese.

To make pesto, blend together the basil, pine nuts and garlic in a food processor or mortar and pestle, gradually adding the oil. Stir in the grated Parmesan cheese.

This will keep in the fridge, covered with a thin film of oil, for weeks.

### NOTE
If you want a more substantial soup, add a tin of cooked, drained cannellini beans at the end, heating them through in the soup.

# Potato gnocchi with duck and blackberry sauce
## SERVES 4-8

*Gnocchi has to be light to eat, to win fans. It makes an excellent first course and also a satisfying main dish for supper. Blackberries paired with duck help balance the meat's richness, and are the perfect partners for this potato dish. If you have a wild duck, it would be an excellent way to use it in this sauce, otherwise one larger duck breast will do.*

200 g (7 oz) plain flour

500 g (1 lb 2 oz) floury potatoes

salt and pepper

50 g (1¾ oz) butter

SAUCE

1 stick celery

1 carrot

1 onion

1 bay leaf

½ glass red wine

1 garlic clove

olive oil

250 g (9 oz) blackberries

250 g (9 oz) duck meat
   e.g. breasts

200 ml (7 fl oz) poultry stock

1 tbs chopped oregano or thyme

TO SERVE

grated Parmesan cheese

For the sauce, finely chop the celery, carrot, onion and garlic and bay leaf and herbs. Fry in a little olive oil until softening and golden.

Cut up the duck into small dice and fry until brown, then add the red wine. Continue to cook until the wine evaporates, then add the stock and simmer slowly for 30-40 minutes. Season with salt and herbs. Finally stir in the blackberries and remove from the heat.

For the gnocchi, peel the potatoes, chop roughly and steam until tender, about 15 minutes.

Fill a large roasting dish with water – it needs to be at least 6 cm (2½") deep. Put it on to boil. Warm a serving dish for the gnocchi, buttering the base.

Spread the flour over the work surface, about the size of a large rectangular baking sheet. When the potato is cooked, push it through a potato ricer (or sieve) so that it falls evenly over the flour. Sprinkle the potato with salt and then pour over the melted butter.

Work the flour into the potato using a dough scraper, bringing everything together into a dough ball. Knead gently for 6 minutes. Divide the dough into quarters and roll each into long thin sausage shapes. Cut each sausage into 2½ cm (1") pieces. To add the traditional finishing touch to the gnocchi, press each one with the back of a floured fork, flicking the gnocchi to create an indentation in each one.

When the water is boiling, add the gnocchi in a single layer. The water needs to be simmering gently. When they rise to the surface, cook for a further minute, then skim them off and put into the warm serving dish. Pour the sauce over the gnocchi and serve immediately with Parmesan cheese.

# Game paté with fruity sauce
## SERVES 8+

*This paté is absolutely delicious and especially more so when accompanied by the fruity sauce. Spread the paté thickly on toast, with a little sauce, and serve as a canapé, or as a lunch dish accompanied with good, fresh bread.*

50 g (1 ¾ oz) bacon

200 g (7 oz) pheasant meat
  (about ½ a pheasant)

250 g (9 oz) chicken livers

25 g (1 oz) plain flour

3 tbs cider brandy

3 tbs whipping cream

1 egg

1 tsp salt

pepper

freshly grated nutmeg

Cut the bacon into small pieces and cut away any discolouration or sinewy bits from the liver. Cut the pheasant into 2 cm (1") pieces.

Put the bacon, meat and liver in a food processor. Add all the other ingredients, seasoning with pepper and nutmeg to taste. Blend until smooth.

Pour into a well greased small terrine, about 850 ml (1½ pts) capacity. Cover tightly with a lid or foil and place in a *bain-marie* of hot water. Bake in a moderate oven at 170°C (325°F, gas 3) for 1 hour.

In an Aga, cook in the roasting oven for 30 minutes on the floor of the oven, then transfer to the simmering oven for 1 hour.

The paté is cooked when slightly firm, and shrunken away from the edge of the terrine. Also the juices should run clear when the paté is pierced. Cool, then refrigerate.

Serve at room temperature, accompanied by the fruity sauce, bread, toast or a salad.

TIP

If you want to divide the recipe into 2 smaller terrines, pour the mixture into 2 smaller containers. Cook one and freeze the other uncooked, defrosting to cook when needed. This is a better way than freezing cooked paté, which never has an agreeable texture when defrosted.

# Fruity sauce
## SERVES 8

*This is a variation on Cumberland sauce, with more body to it. This sauce will keep in the fridge for several weeks.*

1 small onion

1 orange and 1 lemon

½ shallot

2 tbs raisins

4 prunes, pitted

250 ml (9 oz) cranberry sauce

1 tsp crushed white peppercorns

3 tbs pine nuts or chopped almonds

¼ tsp French mustard

Peel and quarter the onion, and leave to soak in water for 1 hour.

Peel the orange and lemon skin and cut these into julienne, then squeeze the juices. Finely chop the shallot. Put the peel, juice and shallot in a small saucepan and add the prunes and raisins. Barely cover with water and simmer slowly for 20 minutes, until everything is softening and most of the liquid has evaporated.

Roughly chop the cooked ingredients in a food processor. Drain the onion and add to the food processor with the nuts. Process again. Finally stir in the cranberry sauce, peppercorns and mustard. Refrigerate until ready to use.

# Blue cheese and apple soufflés
## SERVES 8

*This is a twice-baked soufflé. Perfect for entertaining as you do the time-consuming work earlier in the day and just reheat the soufflés when you are ready to eat.*

100 g (3½ oz) butter

1 apple

50 g (1¾ oz) plain flour

300 ml (½ pt) milk

100 g (3½ oz) blue cheese, e.g. Shropshire Blue

4 egg yolks

4 egg whites

**TO SERVE**

salad leaves dressed with balsamic vinegar

toasted walnuts

Peel, core and finely chop an apple and gently cook in a third of the butter, in a small covered saucepan, until soft, for approximately 5 minutes.

Remove the apples with a slotted spoon. Add the remaining butter to the pan and return to the heat. When it is melted, stir in the flour. Cook this roux for a minute and then remove from the heat. Whisk in the milk gradually. Return to the heat and stir until thick and smooth and the mixture boils.

Crumble the cheese into the saucepan, away from the heat, then add the apple and egg yolks, stirring everything together.

Brush each 100 g (3½ oz) ramekin with melted butter and then dust with flour. Place the ramekins on a baking sheet.

Whip the egg whites until firm and then stir a little into the base mixture. Tip this back into the whites and gently fold together. Spoon the mixture into the ramekins.

Bake at 180°C (350°F, gas 4) for 20-25 minutes until risen and cooked through. In an Aga, put the tray on the lower half of the roasting oven.

Leave to cool for at least 20 minutes before decanting the soufflés, using a palette knife, placing them on a baking sheet, covered with silicone paper.

Reheat when ready to eat for 10 minutes at 180°C (350°F, gas 4). In an Aga, reheat in the lower half of the roasting oven.

Serve on plates, with some salad leaves tossed in balsamic vinegar and toasted walnuts scattered around.

**NOTE**

When preparing the ramekins, be generous with the butter and then shake the flour around the bottom and sides of the moulds. Tap each base on the work surface to loosen any excess flour and then tip it out.

# Wild mushroom salad

**SERVES 2**

*For many years* Cooking with Class *has been taking students on fungi forays. Once you are confident that the wild mushrooms have been conclusively identified as safe to eat, you can enjoy cooking and eating them. If you are not an experienced forager, you should buy your wild mushrooms.*

300 g (10½ oz) mixed wild mushrooms

50 g (1¾ oz) butter

1 finely chopped shallot

100 ml (3½ fl oz) vegetable stock

1 tbs chopped winter savory

1 bunch of watercress or the equivalent of lambs lettuce or rocket

salt and pepper

Wash and dry the salad leaves, remove the stalks and place on a platter.

Carefully clean the mushrooms, removing any dry stalks. Leave any small ones whole and cut up large caps and slice stalks.

Melt half the butter in a sauté pan and, as it sizzles, add the mushrooms. Cook over high heat and, when the mushrooms are golden, add the shallot and winter savory and season with salt and pepper. Cook for a few more minutes, then add the stock.

Bring to the boil, add the chopped savory and swirl in the last of the butter. Remove from the heat and check the seasoning.

Pour the hot mushroom mixture over the salad, and serve as a first course.

**NOTE**

To clean the mushrooms, cut off the bottom of the stems and any dry stalks should be discarded. Wipe or brush clean the caps, wash only if absolutely necessary, drying them on kitchen paper, before cooking. Remove porous spongy base under boletus caps.

# Quick roast pheasant or guinea fowl with chestnuts
## SERVES 4

*The fruity marinade helps the meat stay moist as does the quick cooking. This recipe also suits guinea fowl and has all the echoes of autumn produce.*

2 pheasants or 1 guinea
  fowl

**MARINADE**

50 ml (2 fl oz) olive oil

juice 1 orange

match stick strips of the
  orange rind

sprigs of thyme

2 bay leaves

½ tsp juniper berries,
  crushed

**TO FINISH**

1 tbs dry sherry

150 ml (5 fl oz) poultry
  stock

50 g (1¾ oz) butter

200 g (7 oz) cooked peeled
  chestnuts

2 red onions, cut into
  wedges

salt and pepper

Cut the birds down the backbone, removing it and pushing on the breast bone to splay the birds out. Wipe the birds clean and place in a single layer in a roasting dish. Mix the marinade and pour over the birds.

Roast in as hot an oven as you have – about 250°C (425°F, gas 7) or in the top of an Aga's roasting oven. Cook the pheasants for 15 minutes. For the guinea fowl, continue to cook for another 10-15 minutes until done. Remove them from the dish and keep warm.

Deglaze the roasting pan with sherry, add the stock and put the roasting dish back in the oven for 5 minutes to reduce to a sauce.

Peel the onions and cut into wedges. Heat the butter in a sauté pan and fry the onions with a lid on, until softening, then add the cooked chestnuts and a splash of sherry. Pour on the deglazed pan juices. Check the seasoning.

Cut the guinea fowl or pheasants into four pieces, breasts and legs. Add them to the sauté pan with the sauce. Accompany with some cooked spinach or cabbage, lightly sautéed in a little butter.

**NOTE**
You can buy dehydrated chestnuts which need soaking overnight before boiling until tender, for about 40 minutes or pressure cook for 15-20 minutes.

# Ham hocks with tomato and parsnip mash
**SERVES 4-6**

*Ready cooked ham makes an excellent fast food, and by teaming it with the sweetness of parsnips, you create a sweet and salty combination that is very satisfying.*

2 cooked ham hocks, weighing 1.2 kg (2 lb 12 oz) each

1 x 400 g tin Italian tomatoes

500 ml (18 fl oz) chicken stock

700 g (1 lb 9 oz) parsnips

1 clove garlic

100 ml (3½ fl oz) whipping cream

25 g (1 oz) butter

salt and pepper

Put the tomatoes in a saucepan with the stock and boil for 30 minutes to gain a sauce consistency.

Peel the skin from the hocks and remove the meat, in large chunks, from the bones. Add the meat and any jelly that was clinging to it, to the tomatoes, and heat through gently. Check the seasoning before adding any salt and pepper.

Peel and cut away any tough core of the parsnips and slice. Peel the garlic and steam in a saucepan with the parsnips. When tender, purée in the food processor until smooth, adding the butter and enough cream to make a smooth mash. Season with salt and pepper.

Spoon the parsnip onto warm plates and top with ham and tomato sauce. Serve immediately.

**NOTE**

If you buy uncooked ham hocks, cover with stock, slowly bring to simmering point and cook for 1½ hours, uncovered.

# Seafood kebabs with spinach salad
## SERVES 4

*Here's another quick fish recipe. Grilled kebabs only take minutes to cook. Choose the best varieties of fish available on the day.*

500 g (1 lb 2 oz) cubes of
   fish, e.g. salmon, monkfish,
   red bream

4 uncooked, peeled king
   prawns

**MARINADE**

2 tbs olive oil

juice and zest 1 lemon

1 garlic clove

rosemary sprig

**SALAD**

100 ml (3½ fl oz) walnut oil

1 tbs sherry vinegar

2 tsp honey

1 clove garlic

500 g (1 lb 2 oz) baby
   spinach leaves

1 bunch baby organic
   carrots

3 celery stalks, from the
   celery heart

olive oil

**GARNISH**

lemon wedges

Mix the oil, lemon juice, zest, salt and pepper in a bowl. Chop the garlic and rosemary and add. Toss the fish in the marinade and leave to marinate for 20 minutes.

For the salad, wash and dry the spinach. Wash the carrots and cut into thick sticks. Blanch the carrots for 1-2 minutes, drain and refresh under cold water. Wash and slice the celery.

Make the dressing by mixing together the walnut oil, vinegar, honey and crushed garlic clove. Toss the salad ingredients together with the dressing.

Thread the fish on skewers adding a prawn at the end of each one. Pre-heat the grill and cook the kebabs for about 5-7 minutes until cooked through, turning the skewers to do so.

Serve the seafood kebabs with the lemon wedges and the spinach salad.

# Pork tenderloin with cider, cream and thyme
## SERVES 4-6

*Although this sauce is really rich, it only needs a simple accompaniment such as the sautéed butternut squash. It is easy to prepare and serve and ideal for an autumn evening.*

2 pork tenderloins

2-3 tbs plain flour

salt and pepper

sunflower oil and butter

3 cloves garlic

2 onions

1 extra tbs plain flour

300 ml (10 fl oz) medium dry cider, e.g. *Dunkertons*

150 ml (5 fl oz) double cream

4 sprigs of thyme

2 bay leaves

pared rind ½ orange

chopped parsley

**TO SERVE**

½ a butternut squash

1 tbs each of olive oil and butter

Using a sharp knife, trim away any silvery skin from the pork tenderloin. Cut into 1 cm (½") thick diagonal slices and dip them in flour seasoned with salt and pepper.

Heat a sauté pan with a little butter and oil and fry the pieces of meat on both sides until golden, then remove them from the pan.

Finely slice the onions and garlic and soften in the frying pan without colouring. Stir in the extra flour and cook for a few more minutes.

Pour over the cider and cream, add the thyme and orange rind and bring to the boil. Turn the heat right down and simmer for 15 minutes until the sauce thickens.

Return the meat to the sauce and heat through for 5 minutes to finish the cooking. Correct the seasoning if necessary.

You could transfer everything to an oven-to-tableware dish and finish the cooking in the oven at 180°C (350°F, gas 4) or onto the bottom shelf of the Aga's roasting oven for 15 minutes.

To sauté the butternut squash, halve and then peel it first and scoop out the seeds. Thinly slice and cook in a sauté pan with a little butter and oil, about half a tablespoon of each. Cover with a lid and shake the pan occasionally so that it effectively steams and sautés at the same time. Don't overcook or stir too much or the slices will collapse. Season with salt and pepper.

Sprinkle the pork with parsley and serve with sautéed butternut squash.

**NOTE**
Pork chops can easily be substituted. Cut away any skin and fat before browning the meat. You may need more cooking time in the sauce, depending on the thickness of the chops.

# Pizza pie
## SERVES 4-8

*This is a family favourite, which I serve for informal lunches. It also makes a good vegetarian main course. This substantial pie is filled with typical pizza ingredients.*

### PASTRY

250 g (9 oz) plain flour

½ tsp salt

½ tsp caster sugar

175 g (6 oz) butter

2-3 tbs lemon juice

### FILLING

1 tbs chopped onion

1 tbs parsley

300 g (10½ oz) ricotta or
 cottage cheese

50 g (2 oz) grated Parmesan
 cheese

1 egg

salt and pepper

### TOMATO LAYER

200 g (7 oz) tinned
 chopped tomatoes

140 g (5 oz) tomato purée

1 garlic clove, crushed

generous pinch dried
 oregano

50 g (1¾ oz) sliced black
 olives

### TO FINISH

1 x 150 g (5½ oz) fresh
 mozzarella cheese, sliced

1 yellow pepper, sliced

Make the pastry by mixing the flour, salt and sugar together. Cut up the butter and then rub it into the flour. This can be done by hand or in a food processor. When the mixture resembles yellow crumbs, stir in the lemon juice by hand, adding just enough to bring the mixture together. Knead into a ball, then cut in two, one piece slightly larger than the other. Roll the larger piece out to line a 23-26 cm (9-10") deep quiche tin.

In a food processor, finely chop the onion and parsley. Add the cheeses and egg and blend briefly. Season well.

For the tomato layer, beat all the ingredients together in a bowl.

To assemble the pie, spread half the cheese mixture over the pastry base. Arrange the mozzarella slices over the top. Cover with the tomato mixture, then arrange the pepper slices on top, like the spokes of a wheel. Spread over the remaining cheese mixture.

Roll out the remaining pastry into a circle, to cover the pie. Place on top, pressing the edges together carefully. Make 2 or 3 slashes with a knife on the top.

Bake in a hot oven 200°C (400°F, gas 6) for 35-40 minutes, or in the middle of the Aga's roasting oven. Leave to stand, about 20 minutes, before cutting into large wedges. Serve accompanied with a salad or steamed green beans.

# Grilled partridge with grape stuffing and walnut vinaigrette
## SERVES 2

*Wrapping small game birds in bacon and grilling them is another way of keeping them moist. Although boning the birds can be fiddly, it is worth the effort for the diner. So keep this recipe for a* tète à tète *meal so you are not tearing your hair out boning the little creatures.*

2 partridges

1 shallot

1 small clove garlic

50 ml (2 fl oz) extra virgin olive oil

25 g (1 oz) coarse bread crumbs

10 sage leaves

100 g (3½ oz) seedless green grapes

4 streaky bacon rashers

olive oil for basting

**VINAIGRETTE**

125 ml (4½ fl oz) sunflower oil

1 Granny Smith apple

½ lemon

100 g (3½ oz) green grapes

15 g (½ oz) walnuts

Bone the partridges, by cutting them along the backbone and working the knife around the rib cage. Use your fingers to pull the breast meat away from the bone. When all is loosened from the bones, pull away (or cut carefully) from the top of the breast bone, making sure not to break the skin. Lay the birds flat, skin side down. Save the bones for stock.

Finely chop the shallot and garlic and sweat them in half the oil in a small covered pan, until softened. Tip into a bowl, adding the grapes and crumbs. Fry the sage in oil until crisp and add to the stuffing mixture. Season with salt and pepper.

Pack the stuffing into the birds and reshape them. Wrap bacon around each one and pin together with skewers. Brush the birds with a little oil.

Preheat the grill or barbecue to get it really hot. Grill the partridges, basting them occasionally with extra oil, until cooked, about 15-20 minutes, turning them when necessary. Rest the partridges in a warm place, for 5 minutes, before serving.

To make the vinaigrette, peel and grate the apple, and squeeze in the lemon juice. Mix the two together and marinate for 5 minutes. Strain the apple and lemon juice into a jug and whisk in the oil. Season with salt and pepper.

Roast the walnuts briefly on a tray in a hot oven. Add the nuts and the remaining grapes to the vinaigrette.

To serve, place a partridge on each plate, and pour over the vinaigrette. Serve with potatoes and a green salad.

# Spicy beef stew with stir-fried greens
## SERVES 4

*This recipe is inspired by one of the most popular ones from my* Men in the Kitchen's *classes. It has a wonderfully rounded spicy flavour and is great for using a pressure or slow cooker.*

1 kg (2 lb 4 oz) shin of beef, cut into large chunks

3 spring onions

2 tbs sunflower oil

1 onion

4 slices ginger

4 garlic cloves

½ tbs crushed dried red chilli

### SAUCE

700 ml (1¼ pts) chicken stock

40 g (1½ oz) caster sugar

3 tbs dark Soy sauce

2 tbs dry sherry

3 star anise

1½ tsp five spice powder

1½ tbs tomato purée

1½ tsp salt

¾ tsp black pepper

### TO SERVE

350 g (10 oz) large carrots

plain steamed rice and stir-fried greens

Slice the spring onions diagonally, peel and chop the onion and crush the garlic. Cut the meat into large cubes, cutting away any sinew and gristle.

Heat the oil in a casserole and brown the beef in batches removing the browned pieces as you go. Add the spring onions, onion, garlic, ginger and chilli. Fry for 5 minutes before adding all the sauce ingredients and returning the browned meat.

Heat the casserole and when simmering, cover and cook slowly for 1½ hours.

Peel the carrots and slice diagonally into large chunks. Add to the beef and cook for a further 30 minutes.

When the meat is cooked, remove it and the carrots and boil down the sauce for 15 minutes, to thicken it. Return the meat and vegetables to the casserole and reheat.

Serve with steamed rice (*see p32*) and stir-fried Asian greens.

### NOTE

In a pressure cooker, once the meat comes to pressure, cook for 15 minutes. Depressurise quickly (under cold water) before adding the carrots. Bring back to pressure for 5 minutes. Remove the meat and carrots from the sauce as above, and thicken the sauce by reducing it over a high heat.

# Stir-fried greens

SERVES 4-6

*Any leafy green vegetable lends itself to stir-frying. Cooking greens quickly like this keeps their bright colour and fresh flavour.*

4-6 bok choy or a bunch of sprouting broccoli or a bag of greens

2 tbs sunflower oil

salt

Cut the bok choy in half, lengthways, if large. Do the same with the broccoli. If you are using greens, cut into thick slices. Wash in a sink full of water and drain.

Heat a large wok, add some oil and then the drained vegetables. Stir-fry constantly as the vegetables cook and wilt. Don't overcook as it is nice to have a bit of bite, as a contrast to the stew's melting texture.

When cooked, sprinkle with salt and serve immediately.

# Baked quinces with cider syllabub and Shrewsbury cakes
**SERVES 4**

*I am a quince fan and have three trees in the garden. You can serve them in this way, or use them as a tart filling, cut in wedges, or turn them into a delicious jam or chutney.*

2 large or 4 smaller quinces

300 ml (10 fl oz) water

150 g (5 ½ oz) granulated
  sugar

**SYLLABUB**

150 ml (¼ pt) dry cider

1 tbs brandy

the peel of 1 lemon

25 g (1 oz) caster sugar

½ tsp grated nutmeg

300 ml (10 fl oz) double
  cream

lemon juice

Halve the quinces and place them in a casserole along with the sugar and water. Bring to the boil then cover and place in a slow oven at 150°C (300°F, gas 2) or in the Aga's simmering oven for 2-3 hours until cooked through. Test with the point of a knife. They will have turned deep red in colour.

Carefully take the fruit out of the pot and boil the liquid rapidly to reduce the quantity to a glaze.

To make the syllabub, soak the lemon peel in the cider and brandy overnight. On the next day, pour the liquor into a bowl, discarding the peel, and add the sugar. Stir until it dissolves. Pour the cream into the bowl and whisk it to a firm consistency. Refrigerate until needed.

Scoop the cores out of the halved quinces. Serve warm or cold with a little of their syrup and a large dollop of syllabub, and accompany with Shrewsbury cakes.

# Shrewsbury cakes
**MAKES 25+**

100 g (3½ oz) unsalted
  butter

100 g (3½ oz) caster sugar

1 tsp grated nutmeg

1 egg

150 g (5½ oz) plain flour

In a food processor or mixer, cream the butter and sugar together until light and fluffy. Add the egg and the nutmeg. Sift in the flour and mix to a dough. Wrap in cling film forming a sausage shape and refrigerate until firm, about an hour.

Cut off thick slices of dough and place them on a baking sheet covered with baking paper. Bake at 180°C (350°F, gas 4).

In an Aga, cook on the lowest shelf in the roasting oven with the heat shield above.

Cook for 5 -10 minutes until just starting to colour.

**TIP**

You can cut and bake a smaller quantity and refrigerate for 5 days or freeze the remaining uncooked dough.

# Mulberry and lemon trifle

**SERVES 6**

*Where I grew up in Sydney the boughs of our neighbours' large mulberry tree came over our fence. We loved eating them with vanilla ice-cream. So you can imagine how thrilled I was on moving to Herefordshire to find we had our own large tree. It is the last tree to come into leaf in the spring and the last to lose its leaves in autumn. But before that, we pick masses of berries and enjoy them particularly in this simple trifle. Use blackberries as a substitute if you haven't got mulberries.*

10 ladies finger biscuits

1-2 tbs liqueur e.g. *Crème de Cassis*, or *Crème de Mûres* or sherry

**JELLY**

500 g (1 lb 2 oz) mulberries or blackberries

75 g (2¾ oz) caster sugar

2 tbs water

7 g (¼ oz) of leaf gelatine (2-4 leaves depending on their size)

**LEMON CURD**

50 g (1¾ oz) caster sugar

1 egg

juice and zest of 1 lemon

50 g (1¾ oz) cold butter, cubed

300 ml (½ pt) whipped cream

First soak the gelatine in a bowl of cold water to soften.

To make the jelly, heat the mulberries or blackberries, with the sugar and water in a saucepan. When the sugar has dissolved and the fruit is covered by its juice, squeeze the gelatine to rid it of excess water, then stir the gelatine into the fruit until it dissolves. Pour the jelly into a bowl and cool over another bowl of iced water.

To make lemon curd, put the egg, lemon zest, juice and sugar in a small saucepan. Whisk constantly over a medium heat, until it comes to the boil and thickens. Cook for a further 1 minute. Off the heat, whisk in the butter. Pour into a bowl and cool, then refrigerate.

To assemble, when the jelly is starting to set, break the biscuits into the bottom of a trifle dish or at the bottom of serving glasses. Sprinkle over a little liquor then spoon over the setting jelly. When set, spoon on a little lemon curd. Spoon over some lightly whipped cream and serve.

**NOTE**

You can substitute leaf gelatine with powdered gelatine. Soak 2 teaspoons of powder in half a cup of cold water. When swollen, melt over a pot of hot water before stirring into the fruit.

# Pistachio cones with grapes

**SERVES 6**

*These delicate cones, filled with a mixture of cream and yoghurt, make a light ending to a meal. Grapes are at their best in the autumn so why not celebrate by using them in this dessert?*

25 g (1 oz) peeled
    pistachios (unsalted)

50 g (1¾ oz) icing sugar

25 g (1 oz) plain flour

25 g (1 oz) melted butter

2 tbs crème fraîche

2 tbs egg white

1 tbs Cognac

**FILLING**

150 ml (¼ pt) whipped
    cream

150 ml (¼ pt) thick natural
    yoghurt

black and green grapes,
    quartered and pips
    removed

1 tbs finely chopped
    pistachios

Finely grind the pistachios in a processor, along with the sugar and flour. Pour in the melted butter, crème fraîche, egg whites and Cognac. Process to mix.

Drop a dessertspoon of the mixture onto a baking sheet lined with *Bakewell* paper, leaving plenty of space for them to spread as they cook. Using the back of the spoon, spread the mixture out into a thin circle, approximately 13 cm (5") across. Bake at 190°C, (375°F, gas 5) for 8 minutes. In an Aga, slide the tray onto the lowest shelf of the roasting oven.

When they are golden around the edges, remove the tray from the oven and roll up the biscuits quickly, around a cornet mould. Leave to cool.

Fold the whipped cream and yoghurt together, spoon into a piping bag and fill the cones. Decorate with the grape quarters and remaining pistachios.

**NOTE**

When baking the biscuits, cook 2 at a time, putting a new tray into the oven every 5 minutes. This will give you time to roll up the biscuits before they cool. They will crack if not rolled when hot and supple.

Store the unfilled biscuits an air-tight tin for up to 5 days.

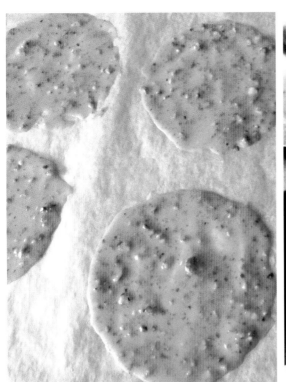

# Brandy chocolate cake with autumn raspberries
## SERVES 4+

*Can you have too many chocolate cakes in one recipe book? I hope not, as I couldn't resist this one. It makes a superb dessert for chocolate lovers and it is enhanced when served with autumn raspberries. These raspberries are prolific fruit producers and need very little attention except cutting to the ground in February, no staking, no watering, just picking from the end of August to the end of October. Couldn't be a better indulgence.*

125 g (4½ oz) dark chocolate (at least 60%)

50 ml (2 fl oz) brandy

1 tsp instant coffee

125 g (4½ oz) unsalted butter

2 eggs

25 g (1 oz) caster sugar

25 g (1 oz) plain flour

**SAUCE**

200 g (7 oz) raspberries

1 tbs caster sugar

**GARNISH**

100 g (3½ oz) raspberries

whipped cream or crème fraîche

Put the chocolate and brandy in a heavy bottomed saucepan with the instant coffee. Over a very gentle heat, melt the chocolate. Stir occasionally, making sure it doesn't boil. Once the chocolate has almost melted, remove it from the heat, stir in the butter, cut into pieces, and let it melt.

Separate the eggs, placing the whites in a clean bowl and stir the yolks into the chocolate mixture.

Beat the whites until stiff, then add the sugar, one spoonful at a time, beating constantly so that the whites are firm and glossy. Sieve in the flour and start to fold it in. Pour in the chocolate mixture and fold in carefully until just mixed.

Pour the cake mixture into a greased 20 cm (8") cake tin. Bake at 200°C (400°F, gas 6) for 20 minutes. In an Aga, place the cake in the lower part of the roasting oven. Keep an eye on the cake and, if necessary, cover loosely with foil to avoid burning. The cake should be set, coming away from the sides of the tin and with a little cracking on the surface. It should be a moist cake, so don't be tempted to cook it for any longer.

Remove from the oven and, after 5 minutes, remove from the tin and leave to cool.

For the sauce, blend the raspberries with sugar to taste. Push through a sieve to remove the seeds.

To serve, place wedges of cake on dessert plates. Spoon around a little raspberry sauce and add some fresh raspberries to the plate. Finish with a dollop of crème fraîche or lightly whipped cream.

# Bohemian gateaux
## SERVES 4-6

*The famous Shropshire damson is in every garden in this part of the country. They have a rich purple colour when cooked and can be used in a myriad of ways. If you have them, use them for this sauce, otherwise use whatever plum you can get your hands on. It is easiest to cook damsons whole and then push them through a Mouli sieve to get rid of the stones. These hearty yeasty cakes are perfect for colder evenings and should be served warm.*

### DOUGH

200 g (7 oz) plain flour

1 x 7 g (¼ oz) sachet fast action dried yeast

150 ml (5 fl oz) lukewarm milk

1 tbs soft butter

1 tbs caster sugar

pinch salt

grated rind of ¼ lemon

1 egg

### SAUCE

300 g (10 oz) plums e.g. damsons

grated rind of ½ lemon

pinch cinnamon

caster sugar to taste

### FILLING

250 g (9 oz) curd or cottage cheese

grated rind of 1 lemon

2 tbs caster sugar

Put all the ingredients for the dough into a bowl and stir together with a wooden spoon. Beat vigorously for a minute then cover with cling film and leave to prove and double in size for about 1 hour.

Melt some extra butter in a frying pan and add a tablespoon of sunflower oil. Using two dessert spoons, form circles of batter, like drop scones. Turn them over as they brown, flattening them slightly with the back of a palette knife. Cook them for about 3 minutes on both sides, until risen and golden.

Stew the plums with just enough water, until they soften. Sweeten to taste with sugar. Cool, removing the stones, then purée. For damsons, remove the stones by pushing the fruit through a *Mouli* sieve.

For the filling, sieve the curd cheese into a bowl and stir together with all the other ingredients.

For each person, serve two warm cakes sandwiched together with the curd cheese and dusted with icing sugar. Pour a little of the plum purée around the Bohemian gateaux.

### GETTING AHEAD

Make the plum purée days ahead and make the curd filling a day ahead and keep them in the fridge. The cakes have to be cooked when you are ready to eat but the dough can be made on the day and left in the fridge until you are ready to cook them.

# Apple and spice cookies

MAKES 20

*Home-made biscuits beat shop-bought any day but sadly not many people bother to make them these days. They need not take up a lot of your time and they are always appreciated.*

100 g (3½ oz) dried apples

125 g (4½ oz) plain flour

1 tsp baking powder

1 tsp cinnamon

1 tsp nutmeg

50 g (1¾ oz) butter

100 g (3½ oz) brown sugar

50 g (1¾ oz) caster sugar

½ tsp vanilla essence

¼ lemon zest

1 egg

40 g (1½ oz) raisins

40 g (1½ oz) walnuts pieces

1-2 tbs apple juice

Cream the butter and sugars together in a mixing bowl, adding the vanilla and the lemon zest, and then beat in the egg.

Sift the flour, baking powder and spices together, then sieve into the mixture.

Roughly chop the apples, adding them along with the raisins and nuts. Add enough apple juice to loosen the mixture a little.

Drop the dough onto a baking sheet lined with silicone paper and bake at 200°C (400°F, gas 6) for 10 minutes. In an Aga, place on the lowest shelf of the roasting oven.

Serve with tea or ice-cream.

# Apple and chocolate crumble

SERVES 4

*This is really a cheat's pudding – something we always need to have in our culinary répertoire.*

50 g (1¾ oz) butter

150 g (5 ½ oz) ginger nut biscuits

400 g (14 oz) cooked diced apples

2 tbs chocolate chips

Melt the butter and roughly crush the biscuits and stir the two together.

Fill ramekins with apple and stir in some chocolate chips. Cover with the ginger nut biscuit crumbs.

Warm in a hot oven, 200°C (400°F, gas 6) for 5-8 minutes. In an Aga, slide the ramekins on a tray into the middle of the roasting oven.

Serve warm.

# Prune bread served with cheese and fruit
## MAKES 1 LOAF

*It is no secret that I love cooking with yeast. Bread making is a very rewarding activity for the baker and I don't know anyone who isn't seduced by a fresh home-made loaf. Serve this loaf with cheese as an alternative to dessert.*

350 g (12 oz) dried pitted prunes

350 ml (12 fl oz) apple juice

1½ tsp fennel seeds

1½ tsp fast action dried yeast

250 g (9 oz) wholemeal flour

100 g (3½ oz) strong white flour

1 tsp olive oil

½ tsp salt

125 g (4½ oz) natural yoghurt

Soak the prunes in the juice for half an hour, then strain reserving the liquid. Purée half of the prunes and chop the rest.

Fry the fennel seeds in a dry pan until fragrant then grind them in a mortar and pestle or spice grinder.

Put all the ingredients, except the chopped prunes, into a bowl and mix to a dough. Add more water, if needed, to bring the dough together. Knead the dough on a floured surface or use a mixer fitted with a dough hook, until the dough becomes elastic, about 5 minutes. Finally, stir in the chopped prunes.

Leave the dough in a covered bowl to rise and double in size for 1½ hours.

Turn the dough onto a floured surface and gently push into a rectangle. Roll this up into a loaf shape. Lift the dough onto a floured baking tray and place, seam-side down. Leave to prove once more, until doubled in size.

Bake at 200°C (400°F, gas 6) for 20 minutes, then reduce the heat to 180°C (350°F, gas 4) for a further 20-30 minutes. In an Aga, cook for 20 minutes in the middle of the roasting oven, then lower the shelf and slide the heat shield over the top. Bake for another 20-30 minutes. Cool completely before cutting.

Serve with a cheese platter of soft cheese, such as a goat cheese, and a firmer Cheddar type. Accompany with a bowl of fresh autumn fruit of apples and pears or plums.

# Winter

## Starters

## Main courses

## Desserts

# Salad of beetroot, bacon and walnuts
## SERVES 4-6

*Salads can be served all year round and this winter one is delicious as a starter. The bright green watercress sauce makes it mouth-watering.*

4 medium uncooked beetroots

1 tbs olive oil

200 g (7 oz) bacon pieces

75 g (2¾ oz) walnut pieces

1 tbs balsamic vinegar

1 raddichio lettuce or a bag of winter lettuce

SAUCE

1 whole egg

1 small garlic clove

½ tsp French mustard

¼ tsp salt

50 g (1¾ oz) of watercress

125 ml (4½ fl oz) in total of vegetable & olive oil

1 tbs lemon juice

salt and pepper

Peel the beetroot and cut it into big chunks. Place in a bowl, drizzle with olive oil, season with salt and pepper. Roast at 200°C (400°C, gas 6) or in an Aga, place towards the top of the roasting oven. Cook for 20 minutes until tender.

Heat a frying pan, cook the bacon until crisp, then add the nuts and fry for a few more minutes. Finally, add the balsamic vinegar and remove from the heat.

To make the sauce, blend the egg, mustard, salt, garlic and watercress in a food processor. With the motor running, pour in the oil. Add a squeeze of lemon juice. Correct the seasoning adding salt and pepper to taste.

To serve, spoon some of the sauce onto plates and then some of the beetroot, bacon and walnuts. Add some salad leaves and serve.

# Stilton and dried fruit tart
## SERVES 6

*You may think that Stilton and dried fruit are an unlikely combination, but they work amazingly well. I sometimes serve this with a drink or wrap it up and give it away as an edible gift at Christmas.*

400 g (14 oz) packet ready-rolled puff pastry

100 g (3½ oz) dried figs

50 g (1¾ oz) dried apricots

100 ml (3½ fl oz) Port

250 g (9 oz) Stilton cheese

75 ml (2¾ fl oz) crème fraîche

pepper

**GLAZE**

1 egg yolk

Chop the figs and apricots roughly and then simmer them in a small saucepan with the port for 10 minutes until the fruit is soft and most of the Port has been absorbed. Leave to cool.

Crush the Stilton with a fork in a bowl with the crème fraîche. Stir in the dried fruit and season with pepper to taste.

If necessary, roll the pastry a little bigger so that you can cut two circles about 22 cm (9") in size. Run water over the baking sheet and shake off the excess. Place one pastry round on the damp baking sheet. Spoon the filling into the middle and spread it out, leaving a small edge of pastry free.

Brush the edge of the base with a damp brush. Place the second pastry circle on top. Press the edges to seal and crimp it using your fingertips. Brush the top with egg yolk and make a hole in the centre.

Bake for 20-30 minutes at 200°C (400°F, gas 6) or in the middle of the Aga's roasting oven until golden and puffed up.

Serve warm or cold with a salad or a glass of Port.

**GETTING AHEAD**
The tart can be made up and refrigerated or frozen ready to be cooked later.

# Scallop and carrot soup
## SERVES 4-6

*Scallops add a touch of luxury to any dish and this soup is so simple yet sophisticated, it will fit in with any busy cook's schedule. This stunning recipe comes from my friend Gabriel Gaté who has taught Australians how the French cook, for many years. Serve the soup at a posh dinner party.*

400 g (14 oz) scallops

2 carrots

½ onion

1 tbs butter

50 ml (2 fl oz) whipping cream

250 ml (9 fl oz) white wine

300 ml (½ pt) fish stock

1 tbs chopped parsley

salt and pepper

Finely chop the onion and grate the carrots. In a soup pan, sweat the onion in the butter for 3 minutes, covered with a lid, without colouring. Add the carrots and gently cook for 5 more minutes.

Add the wine and fish stock and simmer for 5 minutes.

Clean the scallops, removing the muscle and any black bits, then cut them into slices.

Add the cream to the soup and heat through. Add the sliced scallops and remove the pan from the heat. Leave for a few minutes so that the scallops cook through. Add the parsley and serve.

## GETTING AHEAD
Make the soup base ahead, but leave adding the scallops until you are ready to serve.

# Chocolate breads

## MAKES 2 LOAVES

*This is two recipes in one. To the base recipe, you can add either lime and chilli; or the extra cocoa. We owe the combination of chocolate and chilli to the Aztecs, and it works well with bread too. This would be excellent served with the smoked duck salad. Or for a complete treat, just add chocolate pieces to the mix and spread the cooked bread with Nutella for a luxurious winter indulgence.*

1 sachet (7 g) fast action dried yeast

2 tbs brown sugar

500 g (1lb 2oz) strong white bread flour

1 tsp salt

100 g (3½ oz) dark chocolate, I like *Green & Black*'s dark eating chocolate

400-500 ml (14-18 fl oz) warm water

1 tbs sunflower oil

**FOR CHILLI AND LIME BREAD ADD**

1 lime

1 dried chilli

**FOR JUST CHOCOLATE BREAD ADD**

4 rounded tbs cocoa powder

To form the basic dough, put the yeast, flour, sugar and salt in a bowl. Roughly chop the chocolate and add to the bowl.

Decide on which chocolate bread you are going to make and add either of the additions, but not both to the base.

For the chilli and lime bread, remove the seeds from the chilli, discarding them, and finely chop the chilli. Grate the zest of lime, then finely slice and chop it up, peel and all. Add to the flour with the chilli and stir everything together.

For just chocolate bread, add the cocoa powder to the basic dough, leaving out the chilli and lime.

Add the oil to the warm water. Stir most of the water into the flour and stir the dough together. Add the remaining water if needed. Knead briefly by hand on a floured surface then return the dough to the bowl. Cover and leave to double in bulk, for about 1 hour.

Loosen the dough from the bowl and gently knead. Divide in two then shape into 2 loaves. Place on a floured baking tray and leave to prove and double in size for 20-30 minutes.

Bake at 200°C (400°F, gas 6) for 20-30 minutes. In an Aga, place the baking sheet on the floor of the roasting oven. It is cooked when risen, golden and sounds hollow if tapped on the base. Cool before slicing.

# Lentil paté with fruit salsa
## SERVES 6

*Thanks to my friend Bill Sewell for this recipe. He runs very successful restaurants here in Hereford, and in London, and has a very loyal following. This recipe is an excellent example of his delicious vegetarian food. The fruit salsa is a must to accompany this paté.*

150 g (5½ oz) red lentils

1 tsp oil

1 onion

1 tsp cumin seeds

½ tsp turmeric

½ tsp coriander

½ tsp French mustard

juice of 1 lemon

100 g (3½ oz) pistachios, chopped

¼ tsp chilli powder

salt and pepper

### DRESSING

1 lime

¼ fresh chilli

2 tbs chopped mint

4 tbs olive oil

pinch of caster sugar

### SALSA

2 ripe pears

1 shallot

zest and juice of ½ lime

50 ml (1¾ fl oz) olive oil

1 tbs chopped parsley

Put the lentils in a saucepan and cover with water. Simmer for 20 minutes or until tender.

Finely chop the onion and grind the spices. Put the onion in a small frying pan and sauté gently, with a lid on, until soft. Add the spices and fry for a minute, then add the lentils that should have absorbed all their liquid. Cook for 1 minute and then remove from the heat. Add the chopped pistachios and all the other seasonings. Taste and adjust the seasoning if necessary. Cool and refrigerate.

For the dressing, grate the zest of the lime and squeeze the juice. Put them into a blender with the chilli, mint and oil and blend. Add salt pepper and sugar to taste.

For the salsa, cut the pears into pieces and poach in a little water. If you cover the pan with a lid, they will not need much liquid. Drain, then chop and mix the pears with the shallot, finely chopped, the lime juice and zest, the olive oil and the chopped parsley.

To serve, make 3 quenelles per serving. To do this, dip a dessertspoon in hot water, then scoop up a portion of the paté. Now dip the second spoon in hot water, and scoop the mixture from spoon to spoon making a smooth, neat oval.

Add some salsa and drizzle the dressing around.

### GETTING AHEAD

Everything can be done ahead: paté made, salsa mixed and dressing whisked all refrigerated and ready for serving days ahead.

# Leeks vinaigrette
## SERVES 6

*This is a very simple dish, sometimes called* Poor Man's Asparagus. *It is a good way to dress up leeks in the winter and makes a satisfying first course or supper dish.*

6-8 medium leeks

3 hard boiled eggs

2 tbs chopped parsley

### DRESSING

100 ml (3½ oz) olive oil

25 ml (1 fl oz) red wine vinegar

1 teaspoon Dijon mustard

salt and pepper

Trim and clean the leeks well, cutting off the coarse top leaves. Lay them in a broad pan and barely cover with water. Sprinkle with salt and cook over a medium heat until tender, then drain.

Make the dressing by whisking the oil, vinegar and mustard together. Season with salt and pepper.

Place the leeks in a flat dish. If they are really long, cut the leeks in half, and pour over the dressing while the leeks are hot. Roughly chop the hard boiled eggs and scatter over the top. Sprinkle with parsley.

Serve with some French bread.

# Smoked duck salad with avocado
## SERVES 4

*Rolling the uncooked duck meat in spices enhances the smoky flavour. Star anise has an aromatic aniseed flavour that penetrates the food. The smoked duck is served with ripe avocados – at their best in winter – and an orange dressing.*

2 duck breasts, about 600 g (1lb 5 oz)

salt and pepper

2 star anise

1 tsp dried orange peel

2 tsp brown sugar

hickory chips soaked in water

1-2 ripe avocados

1 Cos lettuce

DRESSING

1 orange

1 tbs of chopped chives

2 tbs olive oil

salt and pepper

Grind the dried orange and star anise together in a mortar and pestle or spice grinder.

Score the duck skin in a criss-cross fashion with a sharp knife. Rub some salt and pepper all over the meat. Mix the spices and sugar together and dip the meat into it to coat. Heat a frying pan and fry the breasts, skin side down, until golden – about 5 minutes.

Line a wok or steamer pot with foil. Drain the hickory chips and place on the foil. Cover with a steamer basket. Add the duck, skin side up and cover with the lid. Smoke for 20 minutes, over a medium heat, then turn the heat off and leave the duck covered for a further 10 minutes. Cool, then refrigerate until cold.

Slice the avocados and wash the lettuce.

For the dressing, grate the rind of the orange and squeeze the juice. Mix with the oil. Finely snip the chives and add to the dressing.

Place some lettuce leaves on plates, tucking in the avocado slices. Slice the duck thinly, add to the salad and sprinkle with the dressing.

Serve as a first course.

GETTING AHEAD

You can smoke the duck in advance, a day ahead.

NOTE

You can buy smoked duck or smoked chicken as a substitute for smoking your own meat.

# Pasta roll stuffed with aubergines and pumpkin
## SERVES 8

*This versatile dish feeds a crowd, whether family or friends and is always well received.*

150 g (5½ oz) fresh pasta made with 100 g pasta flour and 1 egg

### FILLING

400 g (14 oz) aubergine

400 g (14 oz) butternut squash

3 tbs butter

3 tbs olive oil

3 shallots

50 g (1¾ oz) fresh breadcrumbs

2 eggs

salt, pepper and nutmeg

100 g (3½ oz) Parmesan cheese, grated

### SAUCE

100 g (3½ oz) butter

50 g (1¾ oz) plain flour

700 ml (1¼ pts) milk

a slice of onion, a carrot and a bay leaf

salt, pepper and nutmeg

150 ml (5 fl oz) whipping cream

125 g (4½ oz) semi-soft blue cheese

Make the pasta dough, (*see p64*) wrap and rest it for a minimum of 30 minutes, after which it will roll out easily. Roll out the dough to the second to last setting on the pasta machine. Cut each piece into 30 cm (12") long pieces.

Bring a large saucepan of water to the boil, add salt and the pasta sheets. Boil for 3 minutes, then drain, being careful not to damage the sheets. Place them in a large bowl of cold water to cool.

Chop the shallots finely and cut the aubergine into 1 cm (½") dice. Peel the butternut squash and cut into similar sized pieces. In a large sauté pan, melt the butter with the oil and add the shallots. After a few minutes, add the vegetables and sauté for 15-20 minutes, covered with a lid, until the vegetables are almost cooked through.

To make the Bechamel sauce, tie the slices of onion, carrot and bay leaf together with string. Put these seasonings with milk into a saucepan. Add the flour and cubed butter, and heat. Whisk continuously to avoid lumps. When the sauce has boiled for a couple of minutes, remove from the heat. Discard the onion bundle and set aside the sauce.

To the vegetables add the bread crumbs, half of the Bechamel sauce, the eggs and half of the Parmesan cheese. Season with salt and pepper.

To assemble the pasta roll, drain the pasta and overlap the sheets slightly to form a large rectangle on a tea towel. Spread the mixture evenly over the pasta sheets and using the tea towel, roll up the pasta away from you. Roll the pasta from the tea towel onto a buttered baking sheet or oven-to-tableware dish. Cover with a little of the remaining Bechamel sauce, sprinkle with the remaining Parmesan and bake in the oven at 190°C (375°F, gas 6) or the middle of an Aga's roasting oven for 25 minutes.

Add the cream to the remaining sauce and crumble in the blue cheese. Re-heat and check the seasoning. Serve the roll cut into thick slices and serve the sauce alongside.

# Fennel risotto with king prawns

SERVES 4+

*Risotto is the ultimate comfort food, and one of my daughter Frances' favourite things to make on a Sunday night. The principles of risotto making are always the same, but you can vary the flavours.*

*With seafood in the risotto, Italians traditionally wouldn't add Parmesan cheese to this dish, but if you like, serve some alongside.*

1 litre (1¾ pts) vegetable stock

1 small wine glass of dry white wine

4 shallots

2 tbs extra virgin olive oil

50 g (1¾ oz) butter

300 g (10½ oz) Arborio rice

2 large fennel bulbs with fennel fronds

8-10 cooked peeled king prawns

zest 1 lemon

60 ml (2 fl oz) lemon juice

salt, pepper

TO FINISH

25 g (1 oz) butter

Heat the stock in a saucepan.

Finely chop the shallots and sweat in the oil and butter in a second saucepan. Cook over a medium heat until they become translucent. Slice the fennel, saving the fronds, and add to the pan and fry for 5 minutes. Remove the fennel and keep it warm.

Add the rice to the shallots and cook for 2 minutes, stirring and toasting the rice. Add the wine until absorbed.

Add the stock, a ladleful at a time. Stir regularly, adding the stock until the liquid is absorbed. The risotto is ready when the rice is *al dente* and creamy. Stir in the fennel after 10 minutes. You may not need all the stock but the consistency of a good risotto should be fairly sloppy. This will take about 20 minutes.

Remove from the heat, stir in the butter, lemon zest and juice. Chop half of the prawns and stir into the rice. Add salt and pepper to taste. Cover with a lid and leave for 3 minutes.

Serve immediately, sprinkled with the chopped fennel fronds and garnished with the extra prawns.

NOTE

I have discovered that cooking risotto in a pressure cooker takes only 5 minutes. Proceed with the recipe above but add all the stock in one go and cook at pressure for 4-5 minutes. Depressurise under a cold tap. Remove the lid and stir over heat to reduce any liquid.

# Venison casserole with cranberries
## SERVES 8

*I love this dish, it is full of flavours reminiscent of Austrian cuisine. It is also easy to make and looks fabulous, good for dinner parties and family meals.*

1.5 kg (3 lbs 5 oz) venison haunch, cut into large chunks

3 onions

2 tbs olive oil

6 slices ginger

6 garlic cloves

1 tsp each of coriander, cumin, fennel, mustard seeds, star anise

2 tbs plain flour

300 ml (½ pt) red wine

300 ml (½ pt) chicken stock

200 ml (7 fl oz) red wine vinegar

25 g (1oz) caster sugar

salt and pepper

2 tbs tomato purée

300 g (10½ oz) cranberries

3 tbs redcurrant jelly

zest and juice of 2 oranges

### GARNISH

250 g (9 oz) button mushrooms

150 g (5½ oz) dried cooked chestnuts

Trim any sinew and gristle from the meat. Peel and slice the onions and garlic.

Heat the oil in a casserole and brown the meat in batches, removing the browned pieces as you go. Add the onions, garlic, ginger and ground spices. Fry for 5 minutes before stirring in the flour.

Add the wine, vinegar, stock, sugar, orange zest and juice. Season with salt and pepper. Heat the casserole and, when simmering, cover and cook slowly for 1½ hours. If using a pressure cooker, once the meat comes to pressure, cook for 20 minutes.

Add half of the cranberries and redcurrant jelly to the casserole and cook for a further 15 minutes. When the meat is cooked, remove it with a slotted spoon, and boil down the sauce to reduce and thicken it. Return the meat and vegetables to the casserole and reheat.

In a pressure cooker, depressurise quickly (under cold water), before adding the cranberries and redcurrant jelly then bring back to pressure for 5 minutes. Remove the meat as above and thicken the sauce by reducing it.

Check the seasoning adding a little more sugar, salt and pepper to balance the sweet and sour taste.

Pan-fry the chestnuts in butter, along with the button mushrooms and the remaining cranberries. Serve the venison in deep plates, spooning over a little garnish.

# Roast Christmas goose with peppercorns and caramelised chicory
### SERVES 6-8

*You will be amazed at how so much pepper can enhance cooking a goose, but it does. It helps balance the fattiness of the bird, as does having a vinaigrette instead of a gravy. Mashed potatoes are a very traditional accompaniment to goose.*

1 x 5 kg (11 lb) goose

3 tbs mixed (black, green, pink, white) peppercorns

100 ml (3½ fl oz) olive oil

3-4 chopped garlic cloves

salt

6 heads of chicory

2 tbs butter

1 tbs brown sugar

**VINAIGRETTE**

50 ml (1¾ fl oz) balsamic vinegar

150 ml (5 fl oz) olive oil

2 shallots

50 g (1¾ oz) capers

Finely chop the garlic and crack the peppercorns using a mallet or a mortar and pestle, then mix everything with the olive oil. Season with salt. Cut away any excess of fat from the goose. Cut out the wishbone of the goose from under the skin then season the inside of the goose with salt. Pierce the skin all over with a carving fork. Brush the peppercorn mixture all over the outside of the goose. Place it in a large roasting dish.

Roast at 150°C (300°F, gas 2-3) for 2½ hours, occasionally pouring off the fat and basting the skin with any leftover peppercorn mixture. In an Aga, place on the lowest shelf of the roasting oven. After half an hour, transfer to the simmering oven for 2-3 hours until tender.

Test to see if the goose is cooked by piercing the thighs with a skewer. The juices should run clear. Keep the goose warm for 15-20 minutes, covered with foil, before carving.

To caramelise the chicory, split the chicories in half lengthways. Sweat them in the butter in a sauté pan then add the sugar and allow to caramelise and soften.

To make the vinaigrette, finely chop the shallots and capers. Whisk in the oil and vinegar. Season with pepper and salt.

To carve the goose, slice the breasts off the bone in whole pieces, then slice them. Remove the legs and thighs and cut into portions.

Serve the goose with the caramelised chicory, and accompany with creamed garlic potatoes and the vinaigrette.

# Creamed garlic potatoes

SERVES 8

1.5 kg (3 lb 5 oz) potatoes, peeled and diced

1 bulb of garlic

200 ml (7 fl oz) double cream or milk

salt and white pepper

50 g (1¾ oz) butter

Boil the potatoes in salted water until tender, about 10-15 minutes.

Put a whole bulb of garlic in a hot oven at 200°C (400°F, gas 6) or in the middle of an Aga's roasting oven. Bake for 20 minutes until soft.

Drain the potatoes and put them back in the pot. Add the milk or cream, butter, salt and pepper. Cut the roasted garlic bulb in half horizontally. Squeeze the soft pulp out like toothpaste and add half to the pot (you can add more if you like later). Mash everything together, then whisk over a gentle heat until smooth and hot.

Check the seasoning and serve with the roast goose.

# Red curry meat balls

## SERVES 4

*Of all the Thai recipes I have taught at* Cooking with Class*, this seems to be everyone's favourite. It is also a hit with students as it is both easy and inexpensive to make.*

500 g (1 lb 2 oz) minced beef

50 g (1¾ oz) plain flour

3 tbs sunflower oil

2 tbs red curry paste (home-made or bought)

300 ml (10 fl oz) tinned coconut milk

1½ tbs fish sauce

2 tbs ground roast peanuts or crunchy unsweetened peanut butter

1 tsp caster sugar

1 tsp lime juice

### GARNISH

2 tbs chopped fresh basil or mint leaves

### RED CURRY PASTE

8 medium sized dried red chillies

5 peppercorns

1½ tsp ground coriander

1½ tsp ground cumin

2 cloves

2 chopped garlic cloves

1 tbs chopped lemon grass

1½ tsp fresh grated ginger

skin of ½ a lime, chopped

1 tsp shrimp paste

1 tbs sunflower oil

Shape the mince into small round balls, about 2.5 cm (1"). Use wet hands so that the meat won't stick as you roll the meatballs. Roll them in flour, shaking off the excess.

Heat the oil in a wok or broad pan and fry the balls until brown all over, tilting and rocking the wok so that the meatballs fry evenly. Remove and drain them on kitchen paper.

In the remaining oil, stir-fry the red curry paste for several minutes over a low heat, to prevent sticking. Add the coconut cream, stir in the fish sauce, peanuts and sugar. Return the beef to the sauce and simmer for 10 minutes. Check the seasoning, adding a little lime juice and more sugar to balance the sweet, sour, salty taste that is so typically Thai.

Serve garnished with basil or mint and steamed rice (*see p32*).

For the paste, grind the dry spices together in a blender or spice grinder. Add the remaining ingredients and process together until you have a smooth paste.

Any left-over curry paste can be stored in the fridge for a few weeks.

# Pork Orloff with red cabbage salad
## SERVES 10-12

*This is one of my favourite posh dishes for winter entertaining, as an alternative to serving a casserole. Like a lot of recipes for special occasions, you have to do a bit of work to have real impact, but it can all be prepared well in advance.*

2 kg (4 lb 8oz) boneless and skinless shoulder of pork (rolled spare rib)

10-12 thin slices of good quality ham

### ONION SOUBISE

60 g (2 oz) round grain (pudding) rice

40 g (1½ oz) butter

450 g (1 lb) sliced onions

### DUXELLES

225 g (8 oz) button mushrooms

40 g (1½ oz) butter

3 shallots

50 ml (1¾ fl oz) whipping cream

### SAUCE

75 g (2¾ oz) butter

75 g (2¾ oz) plain flour

500 ml (18 fl oz) poultry stock

salt, pepper and nutmeg

150 ml (5 fl oz) whipping cream

50 g (1¾ oz) grated Gruyère cheese

Tie the pork into a firm shape. Season with salt and pepper, and roast at 180°C (375°F, gas mark 4) for an hour or in the lower half of an Aga's roasting oven. Remove from the oven. The meat will be partially cooked at this stage.

To make the *soubise*, cover the rice with boiling water, add some salt and boil for 5 minutes, until most of the water has evaporated. Melt the butter in a casserole and stir in the onions until they are coated with the butter. Stir in the rice. Cover and cook in the oven with the pork for up to 1 hour, until the rice and onions are tender but not browned. Purée the *soubise* through a *Mouli* sieve.

To make the *duxelles*, finely chop the mushrooms and shallots and cook them in the remaining butter, in a frying pan, until soft and dry. Stir in the cream.

To make the sauce, melt the butter in a saucepan. Stir in the flour and cook for 2 minutes, stirring. Do not allow the mixture to colour. Remove from the heat and add the stock, whisking as you do so. Return to the heat and boil the sauce, cooking it for a minute to thicken. Season with salt, pepper and nutmeg. Stir in the cream.

For the filling, mix the *soubise* and *duxelles* together and adjust the seasoning. Remove the fat from the pork and slice the meat thinly, making 20 slices, roughly 10 cm / 4" in diameter. Cut the ham slices if necessary to correspond with the size of the pork slices.

To assemble the dish, interleave the ham and pork slices, sticking them together with dessertspoonfuls of the filling. Reassemble into a loaf shape. Put into an oven-to-table dish or on to a baking sheet. Pour some sauce over the meat and sprinkle with cheese.

To serve, bake the dish for 30-40 minutes in a hot oven at 180°C (375°F, gas 4) or in the roasting oven of an Aga, until the sauce is bubbling and the top golden. Serve the remaining sauce separately.

# Red cabbage salad
## SERVES 8+

*Red cabbage, when blanched, is a good ingredient for a salad and easier to eat than raw coleslaw. It makes a good side dish for the pork.*

500 g (1 lb 2 oz) of red cabbage

200 g (7 oz) winter lettuce leaves, e.g. radicchio

100 g (3½ oz) walnuts

2-3 apples

DRESSING

½ teaspoon caster sugar

3 tbs walnut oil

2 tbs red wine vinegar

salt and pepper

Finely slice the red cabbage, blanch for 1 minute in salted water, drain, refresh and dry. Wash and dry the salad leaves.

Peel and slice the apples and squeeze a little lemon juice over them.

Spread the walnuts on to a baking sheet, sprinkle with sugar and toast in a hot oven for 5-8 minutes until lightly brown.

Make the dressing by mixing the oils, vinegar, and lemon juice. Season with salt and pepper. Pour the dressing over the cabbage and leave to marinate.

Before serving, add the salad leaves, apples and walnuts and toss them together.

# Trout fillets with tomato and chervil

**SERVES 4**

*When I look out of my kitchen window and see that the chervil has survived the winter, I feel a surge of optimism as it signals that we are leaving the grey cold days of winter behind.*

*Chervil is a well-known accompaniment for fish. The leaves, despite their winter hardiness here in the UK, are delicate, which is perhaps why one doesn't see this herb often on sale in food shops. If you plant a packet of seeds, chervil will reappear each year in your garden.*

4 trout fillets

150 ml (5 fl oz) dry white wine

a handful of chervil stalks

1 tsp olive oil

salt

**GARNISH**

2 shallots

1 small garlic clove

2 tbs olive oil

150 g  (5½ oz) cherry tomatoes

salt and pepper

**DRESSING**

a good handful of chervil

a pinch of salt and caster sugar

1 tbs lemon juice

100 ml (3½ fl oz) sunflower oil

Place the chervil stalks in a frying pan with the wine and oil. Trim the trout if needed. Bring the wine to the boil, slip in the trout, sprinkle with the salt and simmer, covered with a lid, until the fish colour changes to an opaque pink. This will take 3-4 minutes. Remove from the heat and leave to stand for 1 minute.

Peel and slice the shallots and garlic and sauté in the oil to soften with 2 tablespoons of water and covered with a lid. Halve the tomatoes and add them to the pan, sautéing them for 2 minutes. Season with salt and pepper.

For the dressing, chop up the chervil leaves and mix with the oil and lemon juice. Season well with salt and pepper.

Lift the fillets out of the pan and turn them upside-down so that you can peel off the skin. This will be very easy.

Turn the fillets the right way up and place them on warm plates with the tomato garnish and the dressing drizzled around.

# Pineapple sorbet with Tozzetti biscuits
## SERVES 8+

*This sorbet is like a frozen winter fruit salad as it has citrus fruit and banana as well as pineapple, which is at its best at this time of year.*

225 g (8 oz ) caster sugar

250 ml (9 fl oz) water

400 g (14 oz) fresh
  pineapple chunks

1 ripe banana

the juice of 3 lemons

the juice of 2 oranges

GARNISH

mint leaves

Make a sugar syrup by stirring the sugar and water in a bowl, until the sugar has dissolved.

Purée the pineapple in the food processor with the banana. Add the lemon and orange juice and blend. Stir in the sugar syrup. Freeze in an ice-cream machine. If you do not have an ice-cream machine, pour the pineapple into a metal cake tin and partially freeze. Take it out of the freezer and beat the mixture with a fork, then return it to the freezer.

To serve, scoop the sorbet into glasses and garnish with mint leaves. Accompany with *Tozzetti* biscuits.

# Tozzetti biscuits
## MAKES 30

*These biscuits are perfect with an espresso or mug of coffee, or served with a sorbet. They also make good presents.* Tozzetti*, which are sometimes called* Cantucci*, are traditionally dipped in* Vino Santo*. They are flavoured with* Alchermes *– a pink Florentine liqueur – otherwise use sherry.*

250 g (9 oz) plain flour

25 g (1 oz) whole almonds

100 g (3½ oz) caster sugar

50 g (1¾ oz) soft butter

2 eggs

15 g (½ oz) pine nuts

25 g (1 oz) mixed dried fruit

25 g (1 oz) mixed peel

a good splash of
  *Alchermes* or sherry

¾ tsp bicarbonate of soda

1 tsp aniseed seeds

a pinch cinnamon

Place everything in a bowl and mix together with your hands, blending in the butter as you do so. Form into 1-2 flat log shapes and place on a baking sheet.

Bake at 170°C (350°F, gas 4) for 30 minutes until risen, just firm and golden. In an Aga, cook in the lower half of the roasting oven. Remove from the oven and let it cool slightly before cutting finger thick slices.

Lay them out flat on the baking sheet and return them to the turned off oven to dry out a little. In an Aga, slide the tray into the simmering oven for 10 minutes to dry the biscuits out.

Cool, then store in an air-tight tin.

# Rhubarb Streusel cake
## SERVES 8+

*As winter is nearing its end, forced rhubarb is appearing in the shops. This is one of my favourite warm puddings at this time of the year. Served cold, it also makes an excellent cake with a cup of tea.*

**BASE**

75 g (2¾ oz) ground almonds

75 g (2¾ oz) self-raising flour

2 tbs brown sugar

125 g (4½ oz) butter

1 egg

**FILLING**

500 g (1 lb 2 oz) trimmed rhubarb, chopped

granulated sugar

**TOPPING**

100 g (3½ oz) brown sugar

75 g (2¾ oz) plain flour

75 g (2¾ oz) cold butter

40 g (1½ oz) flaked almonds

**SAUCE**

250 g (9 oz) pink rhubarb

2-4 tbs honey

To make the base, put the ground almonds, flour, brown sugar and butter in the bowl of the food processor. Blend until the mixture resembles breadcrumbs. Add the egg and mix to a soft dough.

Press the dough into a greased 26 cm (10") spring-form tin. Bake in a fairly hot oven for 12-15 minutes at 180°C (350°F, gas 4). In an Aga, bake on the lower shelf of the roasting oven.

Place the rhubarb in a single layer in a baking dish. Sprinkle over a few tablespoons of water and sugar to taste. Bake in the oven alongside the cake base, until the rhubarb is tender, about 15 minutes, although this does depend on the rhubarb you use.

For the topping, put the sugar, flour and butter in the food processor and blend. Add the flaked almonds and pulse briefly to cut up the nuts slightly.

To assemble the cake, spoon the rhubarb over the cooked base, using a slotted spoon. Scatter over the topping.

Bake again at the same temperature for about 30 minutes, until golden.

To make the sauce, wash and boil the extra rhubarb with ¼ cup of water. When cooked and mushy, stir in the honey to taste. For a smoother sauce, blend the rhubarb until smooth.

Serve warm, cut into wedges, with the rhubarb sauce and some cream.

# Christmas mincemeat tart
## SERVES 8

*Some of my early students in Australia are still using this recipe each Christmas. On the whole, we don't eat little mincemeat pies as part of an Australian Christmas, so this dessert was quite a novelty.*

225 g (8 oz) plain flour

100 g (3½ oz) butter

50 g (1¾ oz) lard

1 tbs caster sugar

1 egg yolk

2 tbs water

### FILLING

125 g (4½ oz) chopped, peeled apples

100 g (3½ oz) grapes, halved

15 g (½ oz) candied peel

100 g (3½ oz) raisins

100 g (3½ oz) currants

1 tbs blanched flaked almonds

grated rind and juice of ½ a lemon

a pinch of mixed spice

75 g (2¾ oz) brown sugar

1 tbs melted butter

2-3 tbs brandy or sherry

### TO SERVE

150 ml (5 fl oz) whipped cream

1 tsp brandy

granulated sugar

Mix the flour and sugar together, cut up the butter and lard and rub them into the flour. This can be done by hand or in a food processor. Mix the egg yolk with the water and stir into the pastry base. Bring the dough together with your hands.

Knead the dough lightly and then wrap and chill while preparing the filling.

Mix all the filling ingredients together in a bowl.

Divide the pastry in two, so that you have one piece that is 2/3 of the dough, and the remaining piece is 1/3. Roll out the larger piece into a circle to fit a 20 cm (8") tart tin. Line the tin with the pastry and pour in the mincemeat filling.

Roll the remaining pastry to fit the top of the tart. Cut out a 8 cm (3") circle from the middle, using a biscuit cutter. Place the pastry on top of the tart, cutting away any excess, and crimp the edges together to seal. Brush with water and sprinkle over some granulated sugar.

Bake at 180°C (350°F, gas 4) for 30-40 minutes until golden. In an Aga, bake on the lowest shelf of the roasting oven.

Just before serving, pile the whipped cream, lightly flavoured with brandy, into the middle of the warm tart.

# Tiramisu torta
## SERVES 8

*Special enough to serve at a dinner party or at Christmas, this* Tiramisu *made in a cake form with a chocolate collar looks so professional you'll be really pleased with the result. Felix is the* Tiramisu *expert in this family and he has passed the recipe on to many friends, albeit without the fancy chocolate collar.*

1-2 packets lady's finger biscuits

250 ml (9 fl oz) espresso coffee

500 g (9 oz) mascarpone cheese

4 eggs

100 g (3½ oz) caster sugar

100 g (3½ oz) dark good quality chocolate, 60% minimum, finely chopped

cocoa

### CHOCOLATE COLLAR

50-100g (2-4 oz) good quality dark chocolate

Make the coffee and pour it into a bowl to cool.

Separate the eggs and beat the egg whites until firm. When they are peaky, beat in a couple of tablespoons of sugar.

In a separate bowl, beat the mascarpone with the remaining sugar and egg yolks. Fold the whisked egg whites into this base mixture.

Place the ring of a 20 cm (8") spring-form cake tin on a serving plate. Dip the biscuits quickly into the coffee and cover the base of the plate with them. Spoon a layer of cream mixture over the biscuits. Scatter over some chocolate. Continue layering biscuits and cheese mixture and chocolate. Finish with a layer of mascarpone and a dusting of cocoa. Chill for at least 5 hours.

To make a chocolate collar, melt the chocolate over gentle heat. Cut a strip of *Bakewell* paper the length and the height of the tin's circumference. Lay it out on the work surface and spread the melted chocolate all over as evenly as possible. Take the strip to the freezer and lay it out to set. It can hang or lie. When firm, carefully take it back to the work bench and lay it out. If too stiff, just lay it out carefully on the work surface. Leave it for a minute or two and it will become more malleable.

Take the set *Tiramisu* out of the fridge and carefully remove the metal ring. Smooth the edge with a palette knife and then lift the chocolate collar and wrap around the torta, chocolate against the *Tiramisu* side, paper on the outside. Refrigerate again until ready to serve.

Just before serving, carefully pull away the paper to expose the chocolate collar. Spoon out the *Tiramisu* or cut like a cake.

# Hazelnut, pear and ginger tart with brandy semi-freddo
## SERVES 8 +

*At Christmas time, when I was a child, I was always given a Chinese jar full of stem ginger so this dessert conjures up good memories. Yes, I love ginger. This tart is served with a* semi-freddo *(a quick way to make ice-cream), reminiscent of that other old festive favourite, brandy butter. It is flattering to know that for some of my students, this pudding has become a Christmas tradition.*

### PASTRY

175 g (6 oz) plain flour

40 g (1½ oz) ground hazelnuts

50 g (1¾ oz) caster sugar

125 g (4½ oz) cold butter, diced

1 egg

### FILLING

900 g (2 lb) ripe pears

50 g (2 oz) stem ginger in syrup

30 g (1 oz) butter

30 g (2 oz) caster sugar

juice of ½ lemon

### CRUMBLE

75 g (2¾ oz) plain flour

40 g (1½ oz) soft brown sugar

40 g (1½ oz) ground hazelnuts

40 g (1½ oz) butter

### SEMI-FREDDO

150 g (5 oz) caster sugar

3 eggs

75 ml (2¾ fl oz) cider brandy

400 ml (14 fl oz) whipping cream

To make the pastry, place the flour, ground hazelnuts and caster sugar in a bowl or food processor. Add the butter and blend or rub in, until you have a breadcrumb-like consistency. Stir in the egg and bring the dough together with your hands. Wrap and refrigerate until the pastry is firm enough to roll out, at least for half an hour.

Roll the dough out to fit a 25 cm (10") tart tin. Lift carefully and fit the dough to cover the base and the sides of the tin. Place the tart in the freezer for 10 minutes to chill.

Peel, core and cut the pears into 2 cm (1") chunks. Sauté the pears, in a frying pan, over a medium heat, in the butter, sugar and lemon juice. Cook until just softening for 4-5 minutes. Leave to cool a little.

For the crumble, combine the flour, brown sugar and hazelnuts in a bowl. Work the butter in with your hands until the mixture resembles crumbs. This could also be done in a food processor.

Pour the pears into the tart. Finely chop the ginger then scatter over the pears. Cover the fruit with the crumble topping. Bake immediately for 25 minutes at 190°C (375°F, gas 5). In an Aga, cook on the lowest shelf of the roasting oven.

To make the *semi-freddo*, separate the eggs, whip the whites until firm, then beat in half of the sugar, a spoonful at a time. In another bowl, whip the cream, adding the cider brandy as it stiffens. Finally, beat the yolks and sugar together until thick. Fold everything together. Pour into a container and freeze.

# Italian lemon pancakes
## SERVES 6

*I was thinking of taking some food to my Italian class, which coincided with Shrove Tuesday, when I discovered this recipe. Everyone loved the pancakes filled with a lemony custard. Did it help improve our Italian? I hope so.*

**FILLING**

400 ml (14 fl oz) milk

100 g (3½ oz) caster sugar

2 lemons

3 egg yolks

40 g (1½ oz) plain flour

**PANCAKES**

3 eggs

25 g (1 oz) plain flour

1 tbs olive oil

100 ml (3½ fl oz) milk

pinch salt

1 tbs butter

**TO FINISH**

extra caster sugar

Make the filling by heating the milk in a saucepan with half of the sugar and the rind of the lemons in thick peeled pieces.

Put the remaining sugar in a bowl with the egg yolks and the flour, and whisk together. When the milk is scalded, strain it onto the yolks and whisk together. Return the mixture to the saucepan and whisk until it boils and thickens. Pour back into the bowl and allow to cool. Whisk occasionally to allow the steam to escape and to stop a skin forming on the custard.

For the pancakes, beat everything except the butter in a bowl to get a lump-free mixture.

Melt the butter in a crêpe pan, over a medium high heat, until the butter sizzles – take care not to burn it. Pour the butter into the batter, whisking it in.

To cook a pancake, lift the pan away from the heat. Pour in a little batter, turning and tipping the pan to spread the batter evenly all over the base. Return the pan to the heat.

When the pancake edges are brown, run a palette knife around the edge, then slip it under the pancake. Turn it over and cook for 30 seconds, then tip the pancake onto a cooling rack.

To serve, place a dessertspoon of custard on a quarter of the pancake. Fold in quarters. Place two filled pancakes on each plate. Sprinkle with sugar and serve.

These are good warm or cold.

# Index

# Notes

### TEMPERATURES

For all the recipes I have used my electric cooker, with a fan-forced oven, and my Nobel – a local Herefordshire-made heat-storage cooker – similar to an Aga.

### MEASURES

All spoon measures are level and metric and all eggs are medium sized: 60 g / 2 oz.

Both metric and imperial weights and measures are given in the recipes. It is important to stick to one or the other when using a recipe.

### INGREDIENTS

Bread, for breadcrumbs, can be whatever you have.

Cream: double cream has a fat content of approximately 50%, whipping cream approximately 35%. If you are using this book in Australia, use whipping cream for double cream in the recipes.

Raw eggs: there are some recipes with raw eggs. Be guided by your physician of any relevant health risks.

Silicone paper, *Bake-O-Glide*, and *Bakewell* paper can be used interchangeably.